D0914374

Store Planning
and Design

HF
5429
N686

Store Planning and Design

by Adolph Novak, A.I.A.

written with James Tolman

Lebhar-Friedman Books
Chain Store Publishing Corp.
A subsidiary of Lebhar-Friedman, Inc.
New York

Store Planning and Design

Photo credits: Nordal Associates, Inc., New York, for Figures 2-1A and 2-1B; Malan Studio Inc. for Figure 5-1; and Morganelli-Heumann and Associates for Figure 8-1. All other photographs and diagrams represent the work of Copeland, Novak and Israel, P.C.

Copyright © 1977, Chain Store Publishing Corp.
425 Park Avenue, New York, N.Y. 10022

All rights reserved. No part of this book is to be reproduced in any form or by any means without permission in writing from the publisher.

Library of Congress Number: 76–56649
ISBN: 0–912016–56–6
Printed in the United States of America

Dedication

To Peter Copeland, my friend and partner.
His passing is a deeply felt personal loss
to me, to our associates, to the profession.

Acknowledgment

The author wishes to express his deep gratitude and indebtedness to his partners, Lawrence J. Israel and the late Peter Copeland. His association with them over the past quarter century has immeasurably enriched his experience through team cooperation and mutual exchange of information. The Copeland, Novak and Israel plates which illustrate much of this book represent the results of their untiring efforts and contributions to our mutual profession.

Foreword

In today's world, retailing is a constantly changing scene that reacts to the life styles of its customers and reflects the personality, taste, and business convictions of its principals. In fact, retailing has taken on some of the qualities of "show business" which cast the retailer in the role of "producer."

A store, to a retailer, is a living, breathing, animate setting that seeks to create an ambience and to project an image that will "turn on" that store's customers.

A store should complement its environment, take its place in the community, and reflect the life styles that surround it.

A store must function efficiently at whatever level of service it seeks to offer its customers since, obviously, it is expected to operate at a profit.

As we retailers react more and more to the complexities of our role as producer, it is more important than ever that we work with a crew who can provide the guidance to stage a hit. Adolph Novak has written a good, sound, basic script that should be required reading for all who have input into the production of a new store.

Having known and worked with all of the partners of Copeland, Novak and Israel, I respect greatly the blending of talents that have brought forth, through Adolph Novak, the expertise and common sense of this book. In its field I believe it will become a classic.

Allan R. Johnson
Chairman
and
Chief Executive Officer
SAKS FIFTH AVENUE

Contents

Preface

Store planning and design consist of marrying a multitude of both architectural and merchandising elements to meet the functional, esthetic, and cost requirements of a store building and interior. The purpose of this book is to provide an overview of this marriage, primarily for the benefit of the retail executive who may lack an architectural background, but also for the architect or designer whose experience does not include the merchandising considerations which are the sole reason for the existence of a store. At the same time, it is hoped that the student of retailing will gain from these pages a keener appreciation of the working parts of that selling machine he will one day be called upon to operate—the store building.

The disciplines involved are so varied and technical, however, that no attempt is made here to transform the reader into an expert in either merchandising or in store architecture. Rather, the effort has been to discuss broadly architectural, design, construction, and real estate details of stores as they relate to the merchandising function.

The basic principles are the same for large stores and small, for specialty stores and mass merchandisers, for prestigious boutiques and discount stores, for independent merchants and chains. Only the combination of ingredients differs according to size, function, type, and cost. The quantity and quality of the contributing elements depend on store policies set by various members of the staff within the retail organization, usually assisted by professional expertise from outside. When all the facts are assembled and weighed, final resolution rests with the decision-making top executive.

He must determine whether the architect or designer has been too engrossed with esthetics to consider costs. He must judge whether the store's controller is so geared to reducing expenditures that the merchandising function will suffer irrevocable damage. He must assure himself that the store operations executive has not allowed mechanical and maintenance functions to restrict selling needs and that the merchandising executives have not ignored the supporting facilities so necessary to the profitable flow of merchandise.

The ultimate decision-maker usually has risen to his position of responsibility through his talents for merchandising, finance, and entrepreneurship. He need not be an expert in architecture, design, or construction. The chapters which follow, however, are designed to assist him in the integration of his own experience and ability with that of store planning and design.

Similarly, tens of thousands of small, independent storekeepers face, at one time or another, the problems of opening new stores, of expanding existing stores, or of renovating and instituting functional improvements. Their access to professional assistance versed in merchandising considerations is often limited, and the contractors, carpenters, and woodworking firms on whom they must rely seldom appreciate the retail necessities for various store planning principles. Hopefully, this book will help fill that gap.

Professional architectural and design firms often are called upon to render their services relative to store planning and design. Unless they are thoroughly experienced in merchandising considerations, their knowledge of construction and design techniques cannot be most effectively applied to store buildings. Thus the retail principles included in these pages may help the architect or engineer without prior retail experience.

Finally, students in the retailing and merchandising fields will soon go out into the market. As the builders, planners, and merchants of tomorrow, they will need to be familiar with the elements of design, architecture, and construction, so that they will be able to integrate these elements where and when necessary. It is hoped that this book will give them greater knowledge and expertise in these areas for the future.

Should this book broaden the reader's knowledge and understanding of the marriage between merchandising and architecture which is called store planning, it will have accomplished its mission.

Chapter 1

Planning and Designing Today's Store

Stores are machines, designed to display, house, and sell merchandise. If any aspect of a store hinders any of these functions, it defeats the reason for the store's existence.

This is why store building differs radically from other forms of architecture. Overwhelmingly functional in purpose, a store must be designed from the inside out, to provide facilities for selling, merchandising, and servicing, and to encourage an efficient flow of customers and of goods.

INTEGRATE DESIGN, CONSTRUCTION, AND FUNCTION

The successful merchant is aware of this principle. But unlike the professional architect or engineer, he is not schooled in how to apply it to the design and construction of his building or store. The selection of building materials, mechanical equipment, flooring, lighting, fixtures, and decor elements must be specified in technical terms so that, altogether, they will provide the kind of store that the merchant needs. And in this era of continuing inflation, this must be done without straining the capital and operating budgets of the store.

The architect or engineer, on the other hand, is aware of the effects that his specific plans, design, choice of material, and equipment specifications will have on the capital and operating budgets. He also has an understanding of how these specifications will affect the functioning of the resulting store itself. But unless he is experienced in working for retail organizations, he may be unable to make effective value judgments when choosing between alternatives that may influence a store's efficiency.

Suppose an architect designs the most beautiful store in the world. But suppose that the store's interior does not function for its intended purpose. Despite its beauty, that store is going to fail.

Thus merchandising considerations are an important part of store planning and design. While these may appear elementary to the sophisticated retailer, it is essential for the architect to understand. Similarly, while construction and engineering information will add little to the expertise of the practicing architect, it can help the retailer to better understand the technical ties required in planning his store. Combining these disciplines—merchandising, planning, and design—and understanding their relationship to each other result in effective store planning.

ESTABLISHING STORE IMAGE

Stores vary as much as thumbprints, both on the outside and on the inside. They are different in form and different in function. There are department stores and drug stores, discount stores and specialty stores, supermarkets and shoe shops. They cater to different types of people, attracting secretaries or housewives, club women or scrub women, executives or laborers, and mixtures of any and all of these. They sell different categories of merchandise; from refrigerators to cocktail glasses, from couturier dresses to work shoes, from soup to nuts. Therefore, it is vital to establish, before even beginning to plan and design a new store, the answers to three basic questions.

First, the merchant must ask himself, "Who am I? What are

my strengths as a merchant? For what am I recognized in the community? If I'm unknown, for what do I wish to be recognized?" The store, in appearance and function, must reflect this identity.

Second, he must ask—and answer—"What quality and categories of merchandise do I plan to provide? Am I best equipped to anticipate and serve the demand for one line of merchandise, such as sportswear? Or a broad range of household items, as in a variety store?" The store must reflect both the quality and the category of goods that it actually does carry. It must look like just the place to go for the merchandise carried.

Finally, he must decide, "Who are my customers? Are they young mothers with toddlers in tow? Are they well-to-do matrons for whom a shopping trip is as much a social adventure as it is buying expedition?" The store must provide an atmosphere which the target customer can feel comfortable in, without worrying about being overdressed or underdressed. This means that the merchandise and its presentation must go together, along with being right for the right customer. Plain iron racks are simply not right for mink stoles, any more than plush carpets are for automobile supplies.

Each of the component parts of the selling machine, the location, the design, the materials, and the equipment which go into the construction of the store building must be chosen on the basis of how they answer those questions. In the chapters that follow, site selection, building architecture, exterior design, interior layout, furnishing, decor, lighting, customer service facilities, mechanical systems, and various administrative requirements will be discussed in terms of how they enhance the selling of merchandise. Recognizing their impact is especially important because of the increasing competitive pressures which have snowballed along with the unprecedented retail expansion in this country since the end of World War II.

RETAILING'S HISTORICAL ROOTS

It was not always so. At the birth of the republic 200 years ago, most "stores" were simply sections of tradesmen's homes. Before the revolution Paul Revere's shop in Boston was in the front room of his house. Living quarters for the family and the apprentices were in the rear and upstairs. This is where his customers came to place orders, to pick up finished work, or even to browse among the goods available "off the shelf."

His was no mere mechanic's workshop. Revere's wares enjoyed the kind of acceptance and demand in his own time that those of Tiffany's do today. Even then, however, retail expansion was about to force changes in store locations and operations.

By the early nineteenth century, true merchants began to replace the craftsmen who produced and sold their own wares, and the shopowners who sold their cargos at dockside. These merchants actually purchased and resold the craftsman's entire output and the ship's entire cargo. As they expanded their lines of merchandise, however, they also outgrew the space available in their homes.

At first, the family was simply removed from the shop and installed in a true home on the residential outskirts of town. The steadily increasing stocks of merchandise could then be placed in the former living quarters of the shop. But a building originally designed to accommodate a family—even a family as large as those in colonial times—could not provide adequate space for the widely varying goods which consumers demanded. This need for raw space thus dictated the next move from the former home to larger buildings. These buildings were actually more like warehouses than stores as we know them today.

In fact, the first merchants to make the move bought or rented warehouses. In the coastal cities and towns, such buildings were available near the wharves and piers, convenient to the ships whose cargoes they stored. Inland, they tended to be found along the riverfronts, where the barges unloaded their goods. (Barges provided the most economical transportation of the time.) Thus the early commercial areas, unplanned shopping centers as it were, were situated near water rather than near their customers.

And unplanned they were. Even the first stores that were built on purpose were constructed cheek-by-jowl and copied from the old warehouses that had been converted to retail uses. With the coming of the railroad, however, there was a shift in location from the waterfront to the streets adjacent to the rail depot. Still, it was the convenience of transporting goods which dictated retail site selection through the 1800's, and not the convenience of customers. (It is no accident that both Macy's and Gimbel's flagship stores in New

York are so close to the Pennsylvania Station, as is New York's retail "Main Street," 34th Street.)

Physically, stores began to lose some of their resemblance to warehouses, especially on the inside. Merchandise displays spread from the first floor to the erstwhile lofts, and customers gradually found it easier to pick their way through the stocks of goods and locate the items they wished to purchase. There was little or no formula for the change, however, and many stores, like Topsy, "just growed."

Not until years later, in the retail explosion of the twentieth century, did merchants really begin to analyze the stores themselves; to think of them as machines for selling merchandise. They began using statistics to find out what merchandise sold, and what did not; to find out who their customers were; and to consider what merchandise belonged on the first floor and what belonged on the fifth, what belonged up front near the entrance, and what should be located in the rear.

Prior to World War II, research and theories concerning the statistics of retail stores accumulated at a rapid rate, largely under the impetus of the mushrooming mass merchandising chains. Then after the War came the flood of new store construction with ever-increasing sophistication. Despite occasional slowdowns, this trend shows no sign of ebbing significantly in the near future.

This sophisticated construction today involves much more than the arrangement of bricks and mortar of the store building's exterior shell. It even involves more than the arrangement of merchandise inside. The physical components of store buildings are now subject to increasing subtleties. Technological advances in materials, equipment, and construction techniques are as important as recognizing what motivations induce customers to buy when considering both the design and layout of the store's departments. In fact, such factors even affect decisions regarding how often to change the light bulbs.

Yet important as it is, even a lighting specification may be confusing to the uninitiated merchant. No longer is it enough to say, "I want 50 foot-candles of illumination." For besides incandescent and fluorescent lamps, there are also other indoor high intensity discharge (H.I.D.) light sources such as mercury vapor and high pressure sodium. What is more, you must know not only what kind of foot-candles you want, but also where you want them and what type is most suited to your needs. They must relate clearly to the identity you want to establish, to the merchandise you wish to sell, and to the customer you wish to attract.

Today, successful store design is a form of architecture which, on the outside, reads like a newspaper. When the customer views it, he knows what's sold on the inside, the quality of the goods being sold, the type of operation the store runs, and what economic segment of the retail market the store is catering to.

Chapter 2

Site Selection

Having decided what his identity is to be, what kind of merchandise he will carry, and exactly who his customers are, the merchant knows what type of store he should open to be successful. Now he must determine where the store will be located and what size it should be.

LOCATING YOUR STORE

In selecting a site for the store, the most important questions revolve around the potential consumer market. Is there sufficient purchasing power in the community to support this store? Does the type of customer he's decided to attract have a demand for the type and styling of merchandise offered? Given a significant customer base, what competition already exists? Is there a place in the market for his store? Or has the market reached the saturation point? Having too many competing stores is a real problem in many communities today.

Figure 2-1A Placing a store at the centrally located star offers an excellent potential retail market area, shown by the white boundary. It offers not only a central location in terms of its potential market, but also easy accessibility to the road network.

Figure 2-1B Placing a store here, instead, however, greatly reduces the store's market potential. Since it is removed from the central population, its potential market decreases, as shown by the white boundary. What's more, since the road network does not properly serve this location, the ease of both approach and accessibility is reduced.

Once the location, the market, and the competition have been determined, the merchant must then analyze the accessibility to the store site. The store must be prominently visible to the public, and not hidden away from view. Customers who come to buy must find it easy to get to by whatever modes of transportation they most frequently use; whether they travel by foot, by public transportation, or by private car. If private car is an important means of getting to the store, then parking must be both sufficient and easily accessible. Even the best location in a good market will suffer if not visible or if the customers find it difficult to approach due to poor access routes and traffic congestion. (See Figures 2-1A and 2-1B.)

The exterior design and interior decor must relate to each other and to the merchandise sold and must provide an appropriate total ambience for the goods within. Just as important, the store's location should be the logical place for customers to shop for these items. A spot right next to a rapid transit stop where large crowds hurry to and from work may be excellent for a tobacco shop with goods arranged for quick purchases and high turnover, but it offers little advantage to a furniture showroom in which customers expect to spend more time browsing and deciding on major purchases.

MARKET RESEARCH

Today, new commercial developments are planned on the basis of modern applications of statistics, analysis, and evaluation tempered by experience and past performance. Before plans are formulated, an in-depth analysis is made of the entire concept and all contributing elements. This encompasses the anticipated annual sales of the projected store or stores, broken down into all the various merchandise categories and classifications. The surrounding population is studied to determine age groups, family size, income characteristics, and current shopping patterns. Community growth trends are projected to anticipate future changes. Traffic is analyzed for all hours of the business day to evaluate the existing road network and to determine what improvements, if any, might assure better accessibility.

Major department stores and national chains often will study these functions for themselves, either with their own staffs or through professional market research consultants and traffic engineers.

Smaller merchants usually rely on analyses prepared by or for real estate developers who seek to establish sites for the retail business.

SHOPPING CENTER STORE ANALYSIS

Since the overwhelming majority of sites available for new stores each year are in shopping centers—whether in three- or four-store neighborhood strip centers or in giant, regional, air-conditioned, enclosed malls—it might be helpful to describe the method of evaluating shopping center sites. Market analysts divide the customer base surrounding a shopping center into time belts or zones. These are called *trading areas* (primary, secondary, etc.). The trading areas measure the distance to or from the center which can be traveled by the prevailing mode of transportation within a given time period. Trading areas are not concentric circles radiating from the shopping center hub, but amoeba-shaped areas that reflect the road network or transit system, since customers can travel farther on one road at regulation speed than on another. The zones normally will reflect distances which can be traveled in five, ten, fifteen, twenty minutes, or longer.

The resident and working population within each trading area provides potential customers with differing merchandise classifications. Since few people voluntarily travel more than five minutes to pick up a pack of cigarettes, only those in the close-in, primary trading area are potential customers for our tobacco shop. It is only within this zone, therefore, that the tobacconist need evaluate his competition.

On the other hand, prospective furniture buyers, say, may be expected to travel twenty minutes or longer to inspect and compare items for which they expect to spend several hundreds of dollars. Thus the operator of the furniture showroom is interested in a population analysis of all the trading areas, with emphasis on the rate of family formation, apartment or home construction, and income statistics. He may enjoy some competitive advantages within the primary trading area over other showrooms whose secondary and tertiary trading areas overlap his, but he will want to draw from as wide an area as possible.

The other side of the competitive coin in site evaluation is the degree to which surrounding, noncompetitive retailers complement

Figure 2-2   Mall shops provide a good merchandise relationship when they complement each other. The glassware shop and the adjacent chinaware shop in this mall, for example, both offer tabletop items. (Monmouth Shopping Center, Monmouth, N.J.)

the projected new store. A dress shop and a shoe store, for example, promise to be ideal neighbors for a leather goods outlet specializing in handbags, since the merchandise of each complements the others and in combination provides for better customer pull. (See Figure 2-2.) In this respect, it has been said that a shopping center should be tenanted as though it were one major department store, with the individual shops selected and located in relation to each other as though they were mutually supportive departments. Interior layout (see Chapter 4 for more detail) should be kept in mind during site selection, not only in shopping centers, but wherever multiple stores exist close together.

SIZING A STORE

Store size should be another criterion for site selection, and here is where the store planner and the real estate manager must begin a pattern of close cooperation. Unless it's absolutely unavoidable, the limitations of the site should not dictate the size of the store. Rather, the properly planned store size to meet the demand should be a factor in judging the desirability of the site.

The influences affecting optimum store size are both internal and external. Going back to the market research, what merchandise volume is the merchant justified in anticipating? How often will the stock on the selling floor turn over? How many square feet will be required to accommodate the merchandise necessary to meet the intended sales volume? Regardless, this area should permit the merchant to stock all desired sizes, styles, colors, and price lines to give him a strong competitive edge in the chosen market.

Nonselling functions and services must also be included in his evaluation. Will the store receive shipments directly from suppliers, with ticketing and marking done on the premises, or will this be handled at a central distribution center? Inadequate merchandise handling facilities in the store's back room can create a bottleneck for sales volume which the most inspired merchandising cannot overcome.

NUMBER OF STORE LEVELS

Along with size, the number of levels the store will occupy must also be considered when choosing the site or location. Having a store on one level has many advantages. First, there is greater flexibility for future change, since the merchant may adjust departments and rearrange his merchandise mix as he sees fit from time to time and as the market changes. Second, there is no need to move departments from one floor to another. Third, there are greater opportunities for sales clerks to intersell between departments on one level. This reduces sales staff requirements. Fourth, single level stores usually provide better customer traffic distribution, because everyone enters the store on the same floor. This means that most merchandise is given maximum visibility and better opportunities for purchase. Fifth, a single level operation provides more usable space in the store building and reduces construction costs. Usable area increases as a result of eliminating space required for stairways, escalators, elevators, shafts, conveyors, ducts, and other multiple level requirements. The savings from eliminating these building functions alone is significant. Finally, besides these advantages alone, building code restrictions are usually less stringent for single story buildings, so even further cost savings are possible.

OVERCOMING THE DISADVANTAGES OF MULTILEVELS

Chief among the considerations that make multiple level stores attractive are the cost and availability of land. In large shopping malls, developers are reluctant to lease a store on one level that is very large in area unless it is a major store unit. By splitting the store into two levels in a two-level center, they economize on land area while they increase the number of store fronts on each level.

Of course, there are ways to overcome, or at least compensate for, the disadvantages of multiple level operation. The parking areas of many new shopping malls, for example, are graded or tiered in such a way that half the parking is distributed between levels. This provides entry on both the upper and lower levels, making both levels of a two-story store or center accessible as entrances. This helps the merchant to equalize customer traffic between the two levels. In multilevel stores careful consideration must be given to merchandise grouping and placement, along with the locating of in-store food service facilities, credit departments, and other functions which attract purposeful customer traffic, which will further maximize exposure of merchandise on the levels.

There are, in fact, some advantages to multilevel stores. In large area, one-level stores, for example, customer walking distances are long. In multilevel buildings having the same area as single level stores the floors are reduced in size, thus bringing departments closer together and reducing walking distances. What's more, merchandise groupings can be arranged for mutual support without conflict; fashion lines can be separated from housewares.

Wherever feasible and practical, however, stores should be constructed with the least number of levels possible. In my experience, I have found that as much as six percent of the total area can be gained for profitable use when a planned three-story building is reduced to two. This is generated by a reduction in the multiple building functions required on each level. Thus the salvaged area can be utilized for selling and may significantly increase sales volume.

FUTURE EXPANSION

In determining site location, store size, and number of levels, the merchant must also remember to take into consideration future growth. With proper market statistics and the history of population and economic growth, future expansion plans should be a part of the initial store planning. If the merchant can reasonably expect to expand his store at a later date when growth demands it, he must consider the needs at this stage, especially if later expansion is apt to be prohibitive in cost or simply not feasible. (Chapter 15 will deal with methods of providing for future alterations and expansion at the time the store is planned.)

SUBDIVIDING STORE AREA BY FUNCTION

An analysis of store area is required to formulate initial plans. The area is divided into three categories: building function areas, nonselling areas, and selling areas. The gross area is the total store, 100% of the area enclosed by the building shell (including the periphery walls). Building function areas include walls, entrances, elevators, escalators, stairways, building equipment rooms, shafts, columns, etc. Subtracting these from the gross area leaves an area to be divided between selling and nonselling functions. Nonselling areas include receiving and marking rooms, baling, employee lockers and facilities, offices, storage, maintenance, and display shops, the first aid room—any area, in fact, devoted to support sales whose purpose is other than direct sales of merchandise to the customer.

Deducting this, the merchant is left with his net sales area, the space up front that is primarily accessible to the customer. This includes the public aisles, the space occupied by fixtures, fitting rooms, and, usually, peripheral stock rooms adjacent to the sales floor and accessible to the sales clerks. Stock rooms remote from the selling area are considered warehouse space and are not included within the sales area consideration. Fringe selling areas include such functions as alteration rooms. Some of the stores that charge for alterations consider the alteration room as a selling function; others classify it as nonsales.

It's impossible to set an arbitrary rule for the apportionment of selling and nonselling space. Every retail operation differs in some way from every other, even within chains. There are just too many variables. With the expansion of branch stores throughout the United States, groups such as the National Retail Merchants Association have developed sets of average percentages for selling area. In themselves, these percentages vary by type of store, whether it be a chain store, mass merchandising store, specialty store, or department store.

There are also other area variables among stores which depend upon how the store itself is serviced. If serviced from a central warehouse, it will reduce the need for in-store stock rooms. The receiving of premarked merchandise can eliminate ticketing and marking facilities in the store, thus permitting an increase in available selling areas.

Generally, downtown or flagship stores must devote higher percentages of total area to nonselling and building functions than their branches. They are often high-rise structures with greater area losses due to space devoted to stairs, elevators, escalators, shafts, and walls. Since the parent store sometimes functions as the corporate executive offices, buying office, advertising headquarters, and central billing and credit department for all the branch stores, space must be set aside for these functions downtown, thus increasing the ratio of nonselling area in the branches. Other in-city flagship stores relocate such administrative offices in lower rental buildings away from prime retail areas.

The checklist at the end of this chapter includes most of the functions that require space when considering the building function areas, nonselling areas, and sales areas in the larger full-line department store. While some of these functions are absolutely necessary for all stores, many are required for only certain specialized stores.

DETERMINING A DEPARTMENT'S SALES AREA

Determination of how large the sales area of a given department should be is commonly based on the store's expected volume divided by the intended sales per square foot. However, this is not always an accurate figure. An area located in the center of the sales floor, away from walls that can be merchandised, for example, will usually not accommodate the same quantity of merchandise as an area adjacent to a wall. Goods near a wall may be stacked or hung fairly high, thus permitting greater merchandise density per square foot of floor space.

To a certain extent, this inequity can be overcome through fixturing. (See Figures 2-3 and 2-4.) (For further details on fixturing, see Chapter 7.) But not all merchandised classifications can be fixtured to compensate for a lack of walls. A properly merchandised department provides a depth of merchandise in an assortment of

Figure 2-3 Fixture design and its contributing ambience elements are enhanced today by both wall and on-floor features, rather than by on-wall treatments exclusively. The sculptured on-floor fixtures here create an on-floor shop that displays a specific merchandise classification without total enclosure or visibility obstruction. (Garfinckel's, Springfield, Va.)

Figure 2-4   The zonal plan concept need not be relegated to areas adjacent to the wall only. Porous fixture groupings that provide visibility for the merchandise within the shop can be displayed in the center of the floor, as shown here. In fact, such treatment can even be used to display related merchandise. (Steinbach, Pleasantville, N.J.)

items with a range of styles, colors, and prices that meets customer demand and generates sales volume. It is therefore inconsistent to place the same productive value for all classes of merchandise on all areas for the same category of merchandise when the quantity of goods may vary by location on the sales floor.

Although annual dollar volume divided by average sales volume per square foot is an accepted area determination approach, a truer evaluation of sales area can be attained by analyzing each merchandise department. The method described on p. 77 in Chapter 6 is an accurate and more analytical approach to determining area. While it is time consuming, it will pay off in properly sizing departments where it is applicable. (Some classifications, however, such as notions, cosmetics, stationery, and other miscellaneous small items of merchandise are impractical for evaluation by this method of area determination.)

On the other hand, some exclusive couturier boutiques present only a few items of merchandise. Sizing a boutique of this type is more dependent upon the back room requirements for both fitting rooms and stock, while the forward area is devoted to displays or to customer seating.

The required area for bulk items such as furniture is based on the store's philosophy of presentation. A series of model rooms wherein related items of furniture and accessories are presented occupies more space than a cluster of limited furniture vignettes. Each has bearing on the area allocated.

WORKING WITH REALTORS AND ARCHITECTS

In any store, there must be close coordination between the store's real estate executive, who is responsible for negotiating for the site, and the store planner or architect, who is responsible for putting together a functioning selling machine. For all major department stores, whether freestanding or anchors in a large shopping center, as well as for all moderate sized and smaller stores, such coordination is a matter of course.

For smaller stores, however, this is not necessarily the case. Too often, when real estate deals are made for smaller stores, the store planner first becomes involved with a project when he's handed a shopping center leasing plan and told to build a store within space number 47. There may be any number of limitations inherent in space number 47, from the shape of the space to its location under an escalator well, which, from an architectural standpoint, will make the construction of an efficient outlet expensive and functionally difficult. Still, it is the store planner's responsibility to overcome such limitations. If he cannot, then the store will suffer. Most situations like this can be avoided in advance through early consultations between the real estate executive and store planners.

CONSTRUCTION ALLOWANCES

A final point to be borne in mind regarding site selection is the almost universal practice in shopping centers today of leasing the bare space in which the merchant must construct his own store. Usually (but not always), the shopping center developer will provide a construction allowance toward the interior store construction.

However, this seldom covers the actual cost of completing the store to the tenant's desires. (To understand the peculiar aspects of this "shell-and-allowance" store planning and construction, see Chapter 4.)

CHECKLIST OF FUNCTIONS FOR AREA CONSIDERATIONS

Building Functions

Stairways
Escalators
Freight Elevator
Passenger Elevator
Building Walls
Switchgear Room
Toilets
Meter Room
Passageways
Electric Closets
Sprinkler Shut-off Room
Baler Room
Ejector Pit

Simulated Building Walls
   (Outdoor Shop)
Vestibules
Janitor Closets
Flues
Sliding Door Closet (Enclosed Mall)
Public Telephones
Refrigerated Can Storage
Telephone Equipment
   and Switchboard
Mechanical Equipment Rooms
Engineer's Office

Nonselling Functions

Packing
Receiving and Marking
Fixture Storage
Carpentry, Paint and Display Shops
Canteen Area
Housekeeping
Credit Office
Show Windows
Loading Platform and Truck Dock
Male Employees Locker Room
Female Employees Locker Room
Employees Cafeteria
Employees Cafeteria Kitchen

Dishwashing Room
Protection, Timekeeper
   and Advertising
Time Card Station
Check Room
Paymaster and Vault
Hospital
Office Area
Female Customer Lounge
Floor Receiving and Truck Storage
Sign Shop
General Stock Room
Workshop and Lamp Storage

Sales Departments

Dress Fabrics and Patterns
Sewing Machines
   and Sewing Notions
   (Laces, Trimmings, and Ribbons)

Preteen
Furs
Men's Furnishings
Men's Clothing

Linens
Domestics and Bedding
Notions and Closet Accessories
Cosmetics and Drug Sundries
Costume Jewelry
Fine Jewelry and Watches
Silverware and Clocks
Art Needle
Stationery, Greeting Cards
    and Religious Articles
Books
Umbrellas
Neckwear and Accessories
Handkerchiefs
Gifts and Flowers
Handbags and Small Leather Goods
Millinery (Better and Budget)
Gloves (Women and Children)
Intimate Apparel
Pantihose—Hosiery
Women's and Children's Shoes
Coats and Suits
    (Women's, Misses' and Junior's)
Dresses (Women's and Misses')
    (Better and Budget)
Women's
Junior's
Bridal
Maternity Shop
Blouses and Sportswear
Layette, Infants and Toddlers
Infants Furniture
Children's Accessories
Girls' and Boys' Wear

Men's Sportswear and Casual Wear
Boys' Clothing and Furnishings
Men's and Boys' Shoes
Men's Hats
Pianos and Musical Instruments
Gift Shop
Furniture and Bedding
Unpainted Furniture
Lamps and Shades
Floor Coverings
Curtains, Draperies, Bedspreads,
    Upholstery Fabrics
Pillows and Hassocks
China and Glassware
Housewares
Major Appliances
Small Electrics
Radios, TV, Records
Picture and Mirrors
Curtains, Hardware and Accessories
Wallpaper and Paint
Sporting Goods and Adult Games
Cameras
Toys and Games
Candy and Food
Luggage
Optical and Hearing Aids
Smoke Shop
Beauty Salon—Barber Shop
    (Men's and Children's)
Auto Accessories and Tires
Outdoor Shop
Restaurant

Miscellaneous Services and Departments

Community Room
Prescription Department
Lending (Circulating) Library
Fur Storage and Repairs
Jewelry Repair
Contract Department

Travel Bureau
Post Office
Theatre Tickets
Handbag and Shoe Repair
Gift Wrapping Service

Chapter 3

Permanent Store Components

Proper store planning is accomplished by developing plans from the inside out in order to assure that the store building will envelope a functional selling machine. This fact and the reasons for it will become increasingly apparent as we progress through the evolution stages in formulating a new store. Chapter 2 outlined the basic decisions about interior planning and design that must be considered before site or store location can be determined. Even more in-depth considerations must be evaluated, however, before the building shell plans can be completed.

BUILDING FUNCTIONS AND SHAPE CONSIDERATIONS

Component elements of building functions impose the most rigid limitations on a store's interior planned flexibility. The shape of the building or store, be it rectangular, irregular, a "T" or an "L," cannot be easily changed at later date. It radically affects the configuration of the store interior. Exterior walls cannot be as easily or economically altered as interior, nonstructural partitions. The spacing of weight supporting columns, stairways, elevator shafts, and escalator wells cannot be moved about from season to season with the ease of displays and merchandise fixtures, but must remain where they are initially located. It is within the designated area and with the integration of the multiple building functions that the interior plan and its flexibility must be planned.

Flexibility of structure is achieved most readily in freestanding store buildings that act as anchor stores attached to shopping centers. In such cases the merchant's architect has the freedom to subordinate the construction element considerations to the interior design plan concepts. There is far less freedom, however, within a shopping center, office building, or apartment house where the plans are confined to generally comply with the predetermined construction limitations and restrictions. (This will be discussed in more detail in Chapter 4.)

Shape has a fundamental effect on store planning. Although physical site considerations often dictate the shape of a building, alternative building configurations may be developed for a site. The most economical shape, in terms of construction costs, is the square or rectangle. And in terms of store planning, these shapes also offer a great degree of flexibility. If the building configuration provides areas that jut out as appendages to the building so that the area within the appendage is severely limited, the store planner who places a shop there initially will be faced with severe limitations in the future if the department has to expand. This is why an open area on the inside is the most flexible space.

Naturally, there are stores that operate very successfully within odd shapes, using apses and other restricted areas to locate limited categories of merchandise. This can present a boutique appearance. In fact, many fine specialty shops and department stores use what is called the "closed plan" to purposely create just this effect, since it allows the store planner to work within various configurations. It also makes for a much more interesting and eye-arresting building on the exterior and a more exciting store design than the usual box-shaped square or rectangle. (See Figure 3-1.)

But even the highest fashion specialty store is being built for the next twenty or thirty years, and it's impossible to prophesy accurately how much flexibility the merchant will need that far into the future. However, he can count on the fact that a large, open area, not divided by structural walls or building function restrictions,

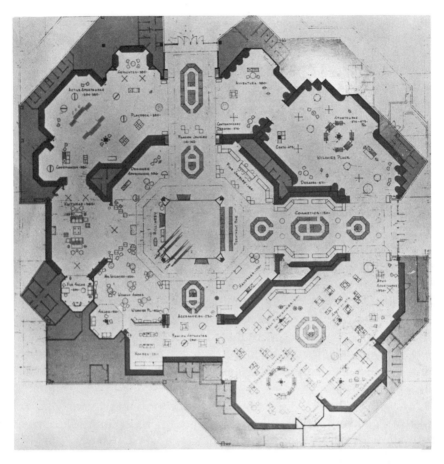

Figure 3-1 Configuration in planning does not necessarily have to conform to straight lines and rectilinear forms. With an odd-shaped plan like this, for example, the varied geometric forms meet various functional and esthetic requirements.

will accommodate expansion or contraction of merchandise classifications much more easily than other shapes will.

The irregular "T" or "L" shapes can offer many opportunities, provided they're designed with care. However, this depends on the size of the store. A "T" shape of 10,000 square feet as an appendage is quite different from one with only 500 square feet. In large stores, a very irregular shape with a vast area in each form still allows tremendous flexibility. In the smaller store, this is not the case. In fact, the smaller the store, the more vital it is to provide a square or rectangular shape structure for flexibility, both initially and for future planned changes.

Stores designed according to the "open plan" (such as most mass merchandising outlets and many department stores) require a single, large, unobstructed area to provide maximum visibility and simultaneously present the widest possible range of merchandise. This, too, is best accomplished in an open square or rectangular plan. (Open and closed plans, along with a modification of both, the "zone plan," are described in greater detail in Chapter 6.)

BAY SIZE

As basic as the shape of the building is in terms of permanence and effect on store planning, the bay size of the structure itself is equally important. A *bay* is the spacing of the columns on a grid pattern in a plan that indicates the vertical construction elements which support the above levels. This spacing has a direct relationship with construction cost. In most instances, the greater the space between columns, the more costly the construction, since the structural members that span this distance are heavier and deeper as the distance increases.

However, the architect must be careful about bay spacing in other respects. First of all, if the building is a multiple usage building with garage space under the retail store, it is functionally best to have the same spacing in the store as in the garage. The controlling factor in this instance would be the space required to fit car widths between two columns. If you don't have to consider the effect of another function such as a garage on column spacing, then you're free to base the decision about bay size on other considerations.

Spacing in a single-level building has a different cost meaning than it has in a multilevel store. In the latter, there must be allowance for a live load of anywhere from 80 to 125 pounds per square foot, if it's a retail facility. Therefore, the steel or concrete structure must have the structural strength to carry that load. The roof live load is 30 or 40 pounds per square foot in most areas of the United States, except in locations subject to heavy snow loads. If a rooftop is used as a parking deck, the roof structure must be designed to support these heavy vehicular loads.

But what is considered a good column spacing from a store planning point of view? Columns are among the permanent elements of the building structure. To begin with, it's helpful to consider the not-too-obvious relationship of the construction of the ceiling to the other elements carried on the ceiling surface. Today's dry constructed ceilings are modulated in one-foot units.

It is functionally advantageous to have a column spacing which will provide a repetitive ceiling pattern that can be maintained from bay to bay. It also is best to provide a bay spacing and a ceiling pattern that will coordinate with the merchandising fixtures and modulation. And since no merchant wants a forest of columns that impede flexibility of departments or visibility of the merchandise on display, he will be careful to space them for maximum visibility. Uniform spacing should be utilized wherever possible, except where there is a specific design need, such as a special major aisle or area which generates a functional reason for changing the uniformity.

Proper spacing of columns in uniform distances can vary from 26 feet to 30 feet or more, measured from center to center of columns. Some planners prefer a bay spacing that is unequal in length and width, thus forming a rectangular bay shape. I personally prefer a square bay because of its inherent flexibility. A square is a non-directional form and provides the planner with more latitude in developing his concept in any direction that makes merchandising and planning sense.

If the planner works with even modules 26, 28, 30 feet or more within the square bay size, his lighting fixtures, floor and ceiling tiles, sprinkler spacing, and mechanical outlet dimensions can be spaced rhythmically into a repetitive pattern throughout the store without change, except for the enclosed plan areas. Uniformity of construction elements will reduce material and installation costs of these components.

Of course, the larger the store, the greater the opportunity for multiple use of uniform materials. In smaller stores and boutique shops, while it is not as important a cost factor as in a department store, it can nevertheless still affect cost savings. Although the number of columns is reduced, the merchant must realize that he is paying a higher premium in structural cost when he increases column spacing from 26 to 30 feet. This is because an increase in column spacing creates an increase in the loads carried by each column. In order to support these increased loads, there must also be an increase in the column sizes, the structural slab reinforcement, and the footings on which the columns rest.

There are, however, compensating factors. Sprinkler heads can cover an area of 80 to 120 square feet. The pattern of sprinkler heads may be increased in larger bays, so the merchant can save on cost. What's more, in open areas, one air conditioning diffuser is utilized per bay. Thus the larger bay means fewer diffusers and another cost savings.

Expert store planners and architects are still debating column spacing dimensions and their relative functional adaptability and costs. The larger bay size is the most flexible; the smaller functional size, more economical. The 26 to 30 foot bay is acceptable in terms of both flexibility and cost. One note of warning: in selecting a column spacing, the planner must be careful that his selected dimensions neither terminate in a partial bay size nor require an excessively longer span than the adapted modulated spacing.

PLANNING A MODULATED STORE

Intrinsically tied to the bay size is the basic store planning grid on which the store's interior is laid out. This will be detailed more completely in Chapter 6, but its function and relation to bay size must be understood here.

Grid is the construction term applied to a repetition of parallel spacing in a building structure. It usually relates to standardization of dimensions, lengths, and widths. It is applicable to vertical as well as horizontal positioning. *Modulation,* which applies to a grid pattern, is a repetition of uniform sizes (not necessarily square or rectangular) that can be interrelated with the building grid. If the building construction conforms to a grid pattern so that component elements of store construction within the grid are modulated, mass production of similar items is possible. This provides a reduction in cost.

Years ago module standardization was not adhered to as a construction practice. Since bays, column spacing, and material sizes varied, they were not adaptable from one area to another. Today's costs, however, have soared well beyond the point where such practice is feasible. Uniform modules, which can be mass produced, purchased in quantity, and quickly constructed or installed have become economic necessities.

Today's construction approach is to adapt and apply grids and their modulated elements wherever feasible. The "skin," or building envelope which encloses and surfaces the building, is modulated; ceilings are modulated in pattern, as are the mechanical systems. Modulation of the construction components and the merchandise fixtures allows the merchant to transplant a fixture, shelf, or hang rod from one department into another without alteration. There is even modulation of the floor and ceiling grids, and of merchandise fixtures and the floor and ceiling components. This permits the separate entities to be integrated.

The use of coordinated modulation permits the merchant to install supporting uprights from floor to ceiling that will support merchandising fixtures or perform other functions. The merchant can install or remove and interchange the upright supports, lighting fixtures, ceiling tile, and air conditioning diffusers from one section of his store to another as the merchandising emphasis changes.

To provide for optimum modulation all component parts of the store construction should fit into the uniform grid bay pattern. The 26-, 28-, and 30-foot bay sizes are preferable because of the popularity of 1- and 2-foot module unit sizes.

The exterior walls of a store building can also be modulated both vertically and horizontally. When the plan grid and the construction elements are modulated as standard components, the whole assemblage will ideally fit together like an erector set.

OTHER PERMANENT FEATURES

While building shape and bay size are two permanent elements affecting the interior layout of the store, there are other aspects of the shell that are equally inflexible. Usually it is economically unsound, for example, to close up entrances and construct new ones at a later date. Similarly, shipping and receiving areas and the loading docks must be planned with care. Even the desirability of show windows is being questioned today. Decisions on each of these questions must be resolved before you construct the building shell.

Positioning of entrances calls for a great deal of analysis, especially of customer traffic and its relationship to the interior store plan. So often, somebody has guessed wrong, and what the merchant expected to be the front of the store became the back, and the back became, functionally, the front. Some major department stores have suffered from such reversals. They placed all their fashion accessories at one door, and most of the customers entered through doors on the other side of the store. It's extremely important to predetermine the flow of customer traffic into a store, because the merchant wants to greet the customers with a classification of merchandise that he will feature "up front."

PLANNING ENTRANCES AND SHOW WINDOWS

In planning entrances, the merchant should remember that show windows are becoming less and less important, especially in shopping centers where there is a captive audience. It can cost as much as $8,000 to $12,000 or more a year to properly maintain a show window, and unless it is kept current, it's likely to be like yesterday's newspaper—dead.

The merchant should keep in mind at all times that his most valuable floor space is on the entrance floor, where the customer is introduced to his store and to his merchandise. If he gives up a valuable area to show windows, where he can offer a limited presentation of his merchandise at best, he's sacrificing space from the highest productive area in the store. And on top of that, he's creating a built-in cost for regularly changing the window display. Thus, as windows diminish in importance, the entrances are becoming even more important in terms of their visibility and the placement of merchandise classifications adjacent to them.

Impact on Security

Entrances must be analyzed from a pilferage standpoint. They are, after all, also exits. This applies to receiving areas, customer pick-up points, employee entrances, shipping docks, and waste disposal outlets, as well as to entrances open to the general public. Techniques for building in safeguards against "shrinkage," as retailers refer to the loss of merchandise not sold to customers, must be considered throughout all the stages of store planning and construction (see Chapter 8).

There are two kinds of pilferage: internal pilferage, or thefts by store employees, and external pilferage, such as shoplifting or burglary, which are acts by outsiders. Regardless of who commits the theft, however, the means by which pilfered items escape from the store is through the entrance. Any unguarded access to or exit from the store is a potential leak in the merchandise pipeline.

IMPORTANCE IN POSITIONING ENTRANCES

Another aspect of public entrances a planner must recognize is that they cut the continuity of walls. This causes a definite division of one area into two. It's difficult for some departments, for example, to straddle an entrance. Fitting rooms or stock rooms adjacent to an entrance increase security risks and often generate merchandising problems. The customer may walk through a department, but the supporting functions must be placed on one side or the other. And if it's a heavily trafficked entrance, the selling department is effectively cut into two distinct parts, neither of which can complement and assist the other as it should by sales staff interselling. This is why, although multiple entrances may seem advantageous in that they disperse crowds and tend to eliminate cul-de-sacs, planners must exercise restraint as well as great care in positioning them.

There is a constant debate over whether a corner entrance is superior to a mid-wall position. It depends, of course, on which way the traffic approaches the store. If the planner forces a corner entrance because people infrequently pass this area, he has created a customer inconvenience to suit his own wishes, thus making his store functionally more difficult to enter. This is the very situation that modern store planning is supposed to avoid.

The greatest advantage to a corner entrance accrues when there is inherently heavy traffic on that corner. (See Figure 3-2.) It then allows the store planner an opportunity to change the planning concept. By using diagonal aisles, he can change the stereotyped square or rectilinear shaped departments into other shapes. (See Figure 3-3.)

When columns are planned for the store on a square grid parallel to the facade, the corner entrance in particular has its drawbacks. A corner entrance on a diagonal facing these columns requires that the diagonal aisle from the entrance be planned between them.

At the same time it is extremely important for an entering customer to be exposed to merchandise by having one department on his right and another department on his left. With this approach the main entrance aisle provides maximum exposure for adjacent merchandise. If a customer walks in through a corner entrance, there can be only a very shallow depth for the departments on either side until he is well inside the store where the departments widen.

Figure 3-2 This illustration shows a mirrored facade with a corner entrance. This provides a visible access from all street corners and is designed to capture the pedestrian traffic from both intersecting streets.

The new Gimbel's flagship store in Philadelphia, however, has a functionally positioned corner entrance. The heavy pedestrian traffic passes that corner; that's where the customers are. It would have been wrong, just for the sake of trying to avoid a corner entrance, to position that entrance elsewhere.

Entrances also affect the positioning of stairways and escalators —two more functions that can restrict interior planning throughout the life of the building. These are component parts of the building structure, and unless they play an important part in the sales functions, they should not be located adjacent to an entrance, since this space is valuable for merchandise sales. What's more, stairs or escalators adjacent to entrances are security risks.

Service stairs should be located on the outside wall of the store. Safety codes require that they exit out onto the street, but this egress should not be for normal customer use.

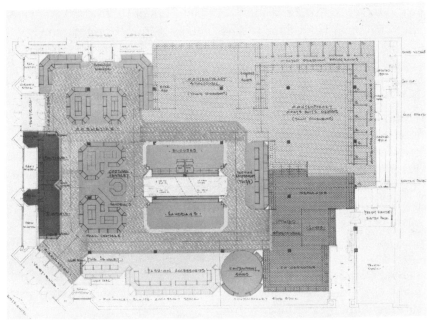

Figure 3-3 This plan provides a major corner entry to the store at the intersection of two major streets, where pedestrian traffic is likely to be greatest. Because the physical area on each side of the entry is limited, merchandise classifications should require very little dimensional depth.

The placement of escalators, however, depends to some extent upon the size of the store. Whether it is large or small, a store should give the entering customer an opportunity to browse through the merchandise. This means that his trip should not be short-circuited going to and from an escalator that is located too near the entrance.

For this reason, escalators should be deep enough back into the store to offer merchandise exposure. In small or narrow stores, they should be placed against the wall to avoid segmenting the interior. In fact, the smaller the store, the more important it is that they hug the walls.

In a large or wide store, however, the escalator location need not be placed against the wall. In fact, it is best centered, becoming an element of the selling function and providing high customer traffic to the sales floor it services. The escalator should be readily accessible to all. In fact, the escalator is the one building element which should be featured, even at the cost of occupying productive space and possibly limiting plan flexibility. The merchant wants the public to see the escalator; he wants them be aware of its location; he wants them to move from floor to floor, since customer circulation is the key factor in generating sales.

While I personally adhere to this philosophy, it is only fair to point out that there are merchants and store planners today who believe that the escalator should not necessarily be visible. There are some stores in which a customer actually has to hunt for some time in order to find the escalator. The theory here is that this search will expose the customer to more merchandise than would a brisk walk to an easily located facility. In my own experience, however, I have found that this can result in both irritated customers and under-populated departments on the upper (or nonentrance) floors. (Many customers refuse to waste valuable time searching for escalators.)

Besides stairways and elevators, toilets, equipment rooms, closets, freight facilities, and materials handling facilities also belong as close to the peripheral walls as possible due to their permanence. This allows a minimum of floor encumbrances that restrict future planning, and insures greater future flexibility.

Fitting rooms, on the other hand, can be more flexible in their location. Normally built of plywood, they can be moved with ease at any time and need not impose restrictions on future changes on the sales floor.

FLOOR-TO-FLOOR OR FLOOR-TO-ROOF HEIGHTS

The floor-to-ceiling height is also an element of the building shell which affects the store interior. In multilevel shopping centers, these heights are normally dictated, even for the anchor stores, since the mall entrances on each level are usually at the same elevation as the mall shops on that level. In a freestanding store, however, the floor-to-floor and finished ceiling heights are dictated by several elements.

For example, the architect will probably plan to place the air-conditioning ducts, sprinklers, and conduits so they are hidden above the ceiling. Light fixtures will be recessed into the ceiling. But the space between the hung ceiling and the roof (or between the hung ceiling and floor of the level above) usually serves as a *plenum*. In addition to being the gathering space for mechanical and electrical devices, the plenum usually also acts as the duct through which the conditioned air from the inhabited area of the store is returned to the air-conditioning system or heating plant. The depth of this space can vary anywhere from three to five feet, and is usually closer to five feet in department stores. Within this space, the architect or his engineer runs horizontally most of the utilities needed to service the floor, and at times the floor above.

In measuring finished ceiling height, compute the distance from finished floor to roof (or from finished floor below to finished floor above), and subtract both the above floor construction and the required plenum heights, including the depth of the finished ceiling construction. The result is the finished ceiling height. The larger the store, the higher this ceiling height should be proportionately in order to avoid having the customer feel as though he were in a tunnel.

As the store decreases in size, the ceiling height can be reduced, but within limits. A great deal of the ambience in a store—the atmosphere generated by its decor and merchandise—comes from the walls and their design and decoration. The lower section of the wall, of course, will be devoted to merchandise. The remainder, along with the merchandise presentation, will contribute to the ambience. Obviously the store designer does not want a ceiling height that, after merchandising, leaves him only a sliver of the wall which cannot do anything decorative or psychological for the ambience. My own feeling is that in moderate sized stores, going below 11- to 12-foot ceiling heights limits design possibilities. If the merchandise is on display as high as seven feet against the wall, there can still be a four- to five-foot-high wall area available to contribute to ambience.

The main floors of larger, multilevel stores, on the other hand, should be even higher in ceiling height: 13, 14, or even 16 feet if possible. It's seldom possible to get that height in shopping centers, since the average shopping center floor to floor height is anywhere from 17′ 6″ to 18 feet. Some areas of a ceiling may be increased in height by stretching somewhat or by running utilities along the walls or sides of an area, but the average finished ceiling height in a shopping center is 12 to 13 feet.

The plenum depth is difficult to reduce, since most stores today return their air through this space, and the volume of air to be handled plus the mechanical service space required dictate the minimum plenum space needed. Returning air through the plenum is one of the most economical ways of both handling the return air and of providing a cooling effect for the recessed lighting fixture lamps. (This increases lamp longevity.)

FINISHING THE UPPER LEVELS FIRST

All of these components of the building shell impose some restrictions on the interior layout and its flexibility for the future. These components vary in importance, depending upon whether the store is to be a single- or a multilevel building. They have a direct impact on the scheduling of the different phases of work.

Often, upper floors are completed before the lower floors. This may seem to be a reverse of common practice, but the concrete floor on grade is generally poured above a mass of conduits and piping which, once covered, can be altered only at exorbitant cost. Rather than hold up all work until underfloor service lines can be finalized and installed, it actually makes sense to work from the upper levels down once the building has been enclosed. Waiting for the completion of the lower floor can delay the entire job. Today, many different types of buildings throughout the world are being built from the roof down by building a center core and working in reverse, a method that has not solved the cost problem, but contains a great many built-in advantages.

Chapter 4

Leasing: Legal Considerations

Most new stores opening today are located in leased premises within shopping centers, office or apartment buildings, or other multiuse structures, rather than occupying their own freestanding sites. Regardless of where they are located, however, shell characteristics impose limitations and restrictions on the interior design of an efficient selling machine. Some of these can be controlled by the merchant, at least to some extent; others cannot. But all must be taken into consideration if the store is to have an effective interior layout, both initially and throughout the life of the lease.

TWO KINDS OF LEASES

Generally, merchants sign either "turnkey" or "shell-and-allowance" leases for new stores in shopping centers. Although leases vary according to tenant-developer negotiations, under a turnkey lease, the store is usually leased fully completed, except for merchandise and trade fixtures. Some leases have been known to include trade fixtures as well. Materials, equipment, and labor are contracted for by the shopping center developer, who does the construction work, often according to the merchant's specifications. Today, this type of lease is most common in smaller neighborhood centers often built on speculation by the developer.

The shell-and-allowance lease, as its name implies, covers a space consisting only of a shell within which the merchant himself must complete his store including fixturization with the help of a construction allowance provided by the developer. Both the degree to which the shell is complete and the size of the allowance vary according to the relative importance of the store to the center and the bargaining powers of the merchant and developer. Indeed, "shell-and-*no*-allowance" leases are commonplace. This is the normal type of lease for mall space in a new, air-conditioned, enclosed, regional shopping center. Obviously, the more the merchant demands from the developer under either type of lease, the more he must be prepared to pay in annual rental.

Under no circumstances should the merchant assume that just because he is signing a turnkey lease, he need not concern himself with the details of store planning. He must be assured that the store which will be delivered to him will function as efficiently as if he had completed it himself. Accordingly, the discussion in this chapter will concentrate on shell-and-allowance conditions, which should be understood by the turnkey lessee.

THE SHELL-AND-ALLOWANCE LEASE

Shell-and-allowance tends to change with the economy. When the economy is off, the number of available tenants is reduced, and landlords or developers are anxious to attract stores, so their allowances and contributions to the finished store space are more generous. When the economy is booming and tenancies are readily available, their allowances are less generous. At the same time, however, some tenants are more desirable than others. If the center is seeking to attract a particular merchant, either because of his standing in the community, because of his promotional aggressiveness, or to balance the merchandising mix of stores in his center, that merchant is apt to be able to negotiate a more favorable set of conditions than, say, the 35th shoe store to sign up.

If the developer is building totally his own center, he may well offer to complete the major department store or other anchor. This is his prime tenant, the main attraction for drawing customers to his shopping center, and he provides many concessions to include this store in his center. At the same time, however, he must construct the overall shopping center itself, including all common areas such as malls, parking lots, corridors, receiving areas, truck docks, community rooms, and the common equipment rooms. In order to build a center economically from which he will realize a return on his investment, he cannot become responsible for having individual stores constructed from individual specifications with individual ambience and individual idiosyncracies. The details would inundate him. Therefore, he does what is standard practice: he approves what each tenant proposes to do for conformity with the shopping center concept and within the center guidelines.

Coincidentally, the great shopping center construction boom in this country has coincided with a tremendously inflationary period for construction costs. During the period in which a major shopping center is actually being erected, from ground-breaking to grand opening, construction costs can increase as much as 10% or 15%. Obviously, leases negotiated before construction begins do not always reflect actual costs encountered before rentals start, unless an inflationary cost increase is built in.

The developer's answer to both the problem of inflation and the physical impossibility of completing as many as 150 individually designed turnkey jobs is to provide only a shell and allow a given amount of money toward the completion of the store by the tenant— a given amount that does not increase with the inflationary spiral.

Probably the most misunderstood aspect of shell-and-allowance deals is the allowance. Retail executives who lack day-to-day involvement in real estate and construction details all too often assume that the allowance will cover the actual cost of completing construction of the store. One of my clients, in fact, an extremely sophisticated and successful merchandiser, signed such a lease, believing that the allowance would not only pay for the balance of the construction work, but would also help defray the cost of merchandise fixtures for the store. He was astonished to discover that the amount was not even adequate to complete the bare store. Seldom, if ever, is it to the desired specifications of the tenant.

It is of fundamental importance, then, that the merchant understand exactly what he will receive under the terms of the lease and how much capital investment he will have to add to it. At the same time, the developer must also understand as clearly as possible exactly what the merchant will require in order to house, display, and sell his goods as efficiently as possible. Today, most major shopping center leases are based on a minimum rental of so much per square foot plus a percentage of the merchant's gross sales volume above an agreed minimum. This ties the developer's self-interest to the merchant's success.

LEASING SPECIFICATIONS

Whatever lease you have should spell out, first of all, exactly what phase of the store's construction will be done by the developer. In the mall store area of a large regional shopping center, this can be as little as "three walls and a place to stand," to quote the construction vice president of one of the nation's largest developers. This may mean constructing separating partitions between adjacent store areas and one exterior wall. On the ground level, it may mean constructing simply a graded area on which a concrete slab must still be poured; on a second level, a structural subfloor may be provided. Everything else, including the finished flooring, must be completed by the tenant.

Some leases call for more construction work by the developer before the merchant assumes responsibility. The lease should pinpoint the exact scope and construction specifications to perform this work, especially on a turnkey job.

Developers' allowances are often tied to specific phases of work which the tenant will allot money for. For bare requirements, they may cover a store front at a given number of dollars per running foot, so many electrical outlets in the ceiling at so much per outlet, a definite type of flooring (usually the most economical) at so much per square foot, and a minimal type of ceiling construction at a specified cost. The tenant, of course, is free to upgrade all of these elements to achieve a more efficient and effective store, but the added cost must come out of his pocket.

One exception to the rule that allowances will not cover the costs of finishing the individual store project, while a rarity, does exist. When a major shopping center developer seeks to open a mall in a new market, he will have a nucleus of national chains with whom he does business on a regular basis. These will constitute a good percentage of the tenants in the new center. Local merchants, however, are extremely desirable to the developer, since he hopes, through his new facility, to change the shopping habits of the area. Since many local merchants lack the capitalization to complete a store with minimal allowances, the developer may cover their full construction costs where it would otherwise be impractical to provide a turnkey job. However, the increased rental plus the tenant's desirability will make this well worth the developer's while.

Normally, however, the landlord expects the merchant to install his own store fixtures. He also expects him to put in his own floor covering, although this may vary. Sometimes the tenant receives an allowance toward the finished flooring, and sometimes the whole project becomes the tenant's responsibility. The landlord will generally be responsible for ceilings, but not finished ceilings if they are to be dropped, or *coved*, with recessed lighting fixtures or other individual characteristics.

The tenant must usually interconnect his store fixtures electrically and connect his own mechanical equipment. He must also furnish and install signs and buy his cash registers. In some cases, he must even provide his own heating and air-conditioning system, with his individual rooftop unit serving only his store. In others, he may tie in with a central chilled water or forced air system provided by the developer for which he pays a utility charge to the developer above his rent, but even here he is usually required to install and maintain his own fans and air handling equipment.

This shifting of responsibility to the tenant also results in a shift of decision-making concerning the finished store's end product, as the developer ceases all finished construction. As in a wholly owned store, the merchant must decide how much he wants to spend. Does he want $9 carpeting or $15 carpeting? Does he want an exposed ceiling or a dropped ceiling? Does he want fluorescent lighting or incandescent? Does he want gentle, hardly noticeable distribution of air conditioning from many diffusers or a blast of cool or warm air from one central diffuser? All involve different cost factors in the planning and design of the store. They will either stretch the allowances from the developer or eat up those dollars very fast.

NEGOTIATING WITH THE DEVELOPER

The tenant finds himself in a very uncertain position when negotiating with a developer. Since the allowances offered by the developer may be either adequate or insufficient, the merchant must be able to interpret what his amount can purchase in order to achieve the store he desires. Alternatively, the landlord may offer to provide certain phases of work instead of an allowance. He may stipulate what phases of work he will provide: 50 foot-candles of lighting, resilient tile flooring, the number of running feet of partitions he will install, etc. These are usually agreed upon before the drawings are formulated.

In my experience, the results of such "blind" negotiations have proved woefully inadequate all too often. In one case, the tenant's lawyers reviewed his lease documents and his contracts to be certain that the developer would provide what the tenant expected. Unfortunately, these lawyers were not educated in the details of building construction or store planning. Although they approved the contract, the tenant later suffered considerable unanticipated costs because of technical misinterpretations.

I have personally had contracts brought before me by clients who had an astute body of lawyers review the contracts with a fine tooth comb prior to having the store's president sign. In spite of this legal review, the contract offered the tenant an extremely vulnerable agreement. For example, the document simply specified 50 foot-candles of lighting. However, it did not state the lighting characteristics; namely, whether it was to be fluorescent or incandescent. It did not indicate whether the fixtures would be recessed into the ceiling or surface mounted. And it failed to specify whether or not the lamps would be furnished and installed by the developer, and whether he would connect the lighting fixtures to the electric service. It even omitted the normal stipulation as to the number of lighting fixtures per bay or circuit, basing it on the local building code, which is often substandard in comparison to the store's requirements.

The lease, which had just been signed to continue for the next 25 years, only stipulated that the merchant would have lighting that produced 50 foot-candles. When these deficiencies were brought to the tenant's attention about two hours after the lease signing, a dispute developed between the tenant and the developer which caused considerable ill will and additional time. This could easily have been avoided had the tenant checked into the matter just a few hours sooner.

DETERMINING THE RESPONSIBILITIES OF THE DEVELOPERS AND TENANTS

The problem facing the tenant at this early stage is whether he will be receiving from the developer what he actually needs to construct the kind of store he desires. The legal documents relate to generalities, but how can he determine his specific requirements?

Obviously, the merchant does not wish to prematurely invest in a set of plans which may cost thousands of dollars before he has consummated a lease. Yet it is imperative that he know specifically what he may expect from the developer. An ambiguous lease that does not clearly define the intent may become the most severe limitation imposed on the store's cost, ultimate design, and future operation.

In order to minimize conflict and misunderstanding between the tenant and the developer, therefore, it is wise to develop an "outline specification" that can be annexed to the lease at an economical cost to the tenant. The outline specification is subdivided into the various phases of store planning and construction. Ceilings, lighting, plumbing, structural work, and materials are defined. It is not a document designed for the tenant to win wars with the developer. Nor is it intended for the developer to use as a club on the tenant. It is, rather, a basis from which differences between the two can be narrowed down to achieve an understanding of the specific phases of work to be performed by both developer and tenant, at least as far as possible without drawings. It is a document that sets basic ground rules relating to the store planning functions which must be developed.

In addition, this document helps the tenant to focus more realistically on his responsibilities, while it binds the developer more firmly to his. Normally, this document is annexed to the lease or other legal document committing the tenant to the premises. Despite the lack of finished plans, it spells out the type of lighting fixtures, the manufacturer or equal, the circuiting requirements, foot-candles to be maintained, the type of ballasts, who will furnish and install the lamps (bulbs), etc.

Such details are extremely helpful, regardless of whether the developer himself does the work or whether he gives the tenant an allowance. If he offers an allowance, the outline specification makes it much easier to prepare budget estimates for the work to be performed. When the developer is to perform the work, a precise and concise detailed description of his responsibilities is available for the store planner, who must incorporate the intent into the plans. The outline specification is not absolutely foolproof; the Constitution, after all, is still being argued in the courts. But it does reduce disagreement, arguments, and disputes after the work is in progress.

WHO DOES THE CONSTRUCTION?

Let's assume, then, that the merchant has received an allowance from the developer, or is responsible, in any event, for most of the construction work to be accomplished inside the store. What, then, is next in sequence? The tenant must select someone to do the work. He may employ the developer as his contractor for part or all of the work to be performed. More commonly, however, the developer will require the tenant to employ his (the tenant's) own contractor. This means that the merchant, with the assistance of his architect, will retain an independent general contractor to complete the remainder of any work that is his responsibility. However, the lines of communication pertaining to the job construction will flow from the developer to the architect/designer as the tenant's representative before turnover to the tenant, and from the architect/designer to the contractor after turnover.

SCHEDULED OPENINGS AND OTHER RESPONSIBILITIES

When the tenant is responsible for the work, he also is responsible for getting the building permits, maintaining files, keeping to a schedule, and opening the store on time. The developer has a keen interest in opening all of his tenancies at the same time so that he can arrange for the Grand Opening of the shopping center. He therefore writes into the lease provisions requiring the work to be completed at certain times, including the specific date for the opening of the store. In turn, the tenant requires that the developer meet such requirements as completing the parking area by a specified time and assuring that the truck loading and unloading areas are ready to receive store fixtures and merchandise. This further guarantees that a certain percentage of the stores in the center will actually open on time, creating an entire shopping center impact, rather than a few isolated store openings.

Thus from the beginning, both developer and merchant are committing themselves to an opening date—usually timed to a specific sales season—when rentals will begin and business will be transacted. This is extremely important to the merchant. He usually buys seasonal merchandise far in advance, so if he misses an intended opening date, he can lose sales which will financially hurt his store from the outset. Many leases specify, therefore, that if work being done by the developer is not completed in time for the store to open as originally planned, the store may be occupied after completion until the following selling season either rent-free or at a temporarily reduced rent. On the other hand, if the center opens and the store is not yet completed as agreed because of the tenant's failure, the rent starts, regardless; the meter is ticking. The opening is so important, in fact, that in Europe many developers provide a rent incentive allowance for opening on time.

Scheduling is especially intricate in a major shopping center, because the merchant is no longer in a world of his own; he is a part of a whole, integrated family of stores operating together. Once the developer has established the date for his planned opening, the merchant should develop a time schedule by working back from the date of opening to set other related schedules. First, he should estimate the time required to 1) merchandise the store once it's physically complete and 2) familiarize the sales staff with both the store's operations and the merchandise prior to the opening. He should then determine how long it will take to install the fixtures which will hold and display the merchandise.

It's also extremely important to determine the length of time required to manufacture the merchandise fixtures; more than one store opening has been delayed because the fixtures were not delivered when the store was ready to receive them. Generally, this happened either because they had not been ordered early enough or because the fixture contractor had assumed more responsibility than his plant could produce.

Finally, the merchant must estimate the construction phases which he is responsible for so that they can be coordinated with fixture installations, floor coverings, painting, decorating, etc. All phases must fit into the time frame between the date of starting (including planning) and the date of the Grand Opening. (Grand Openings are given deference because of the old retailing law that the two best days a merchant ever will have are the day he opens and the day he closes.)

Of course, the tenant's schedule does not take place in a vacuum; the activity on his behalf must be coordinated with that of the developer and of the other tenants. Coordination in scheduling the various trades is essential for installation. Thus leases often require that the tenant be notified by the landlord so many days or months prior to opening if there will be any change or delay because of any one of numerous reasons, including strikes or natural calamities. This safeguard is designed to protect the merchant who will be ordering merchandise, and to assure that fixtures will be delivered when needed, and not delivered to an unfinished building.

SELECTING A CONTRACTOR

Coordinated construction within the time frame is an art in itself. As mentioned in Chapter 3, multilevel stores often complete the upper levels before the lowest level, simply because under the lowest level floor are many of the utility lines and electrical feeder lines that must be installed before the concrete slab is poured. Single-level stores must be equally careful that utility lines and electrical runs are properly in place ahead of the slab installation, since it is obviously uneconomical to tear up floors in order to make changes. Whether the tenant or the developer is responsible for the floor, the merchant must know what is run in and under it, so that he can build in some degree of flexibility for future use. This radically affects what the store planner can do later, should change be required.

When the developer is serving as the tenant's contractor, there are some considerations to bear in mind. In some localities, the labor availability is scarce, creating shortages of manpower in the skilled building trades. The developer/contractor gets his crews from the various trade union hiring halls, carpenters, plumbers, and electricians. While a developer may be sincere and honest, nevertheless his primary interest is to open the major stores and to construct the other component facilities of the shopping center. He tends, therefore, to concentrate on those areas of special interest.

The small space tenant may therefore find he can't complete his work in time because he lacks the leverage to demand the needed manpower more available to the important anchor stores. I have seen operators of moderate sized stores press the developer for weeks to get carpenters or electricians or plumbers, while the developer simply couldn't furnish more men. A smaller, independent, general contractor from the community who has a permanent, but more limited work force with fewer demands can be an advantage in situations like this.

Locating and selecting such a general contractor is important if you face a trying labor situation. The best approach is to talk to other merchants who have used general contractors in the area. The tenant should select a general contractor, rather than a series of subcontractors, in order to simplify his involvement, so that his line of communication is with one firm, rather than with multiple, subcontracting firms. The local association of construction contractors usually maintains a listing of all legitimate firms.

The next step is to identify which of these has experience in retail store construction. The right one should be accustomed to coordinating his work with all the other contractors and with the developer, since they will be performing their functions simultaneously within the limited store area. He also should know the peculiarities of working in store buildings. A contractor who has specialized in apartment house construction has little to offer.

The contractor should even be knowledgeable about the tenant's problems of merchandising, especially in the later stages of completion when the final construction work may overlap with the merchandise stocking of the store. He must understand the overriding importance of sticking to schedules and completing the store on time for opening date. The contractor's knowledge of store operations is particularly important when store alterations occur, to help keep the store in business during construction. By all means, the merchant should search out other store owners for whom the contractor has done work and make sure that he maintained his schedule and performed in a qualified manner, that he didn't overcharge with "extras," that he provided sufficient manpower, and that he properly supervised his own men and those of the subcontractor.

So much for opening a store in newly constructed facilities such as shopping centers. A significant number of stores each year open in existing buildings, either in takeover locations where another store has closed, or in spaces previously used for other than retail purposes.

CONSTRUCTING OR ALTERING STORES IN EXISTING STRUCTURES

When planning a store in existing structures, the merchant must be extremely careful in his approach. If there are existing plans available, he has at least some indication of the conditions within the demised (transferred) premises. These should be checked against the conditions at the site. Often building changes are not reflected on the plans. The walls in an existing building often hide what is behind and inside them. In general, the older the building, the more unknowns exist, but even in newer buildings, "as is construction" can vary from even the last and so-called "final" drawing on file.

Contractors will usually be reluctant to commit themselves to firm prices for work to be done with all of these unknowns, which can affect the mechanical systems, piping, wiring, heating, air conditioning, and other structural and building functions. Most construction firms will contract such jobs only with the understanding that they will be executed on a cost plus fee basis. Honest contractors will take pains to explore the field conditions to assure that the merchant understands the risks. Others will simply present him with the costs as they are encountered.

If there are existing drawings, the merchant or his technical representative should analyze them, evaluate their adaptation to the store desired, investigate the condition in the field, and try to check whether there have been any changes made from what is indicated on them. Should no drawings be available, he can dig test pits, open holes here and there in the wall and the ceiling, explore the space above the ceiling, and try to get the best picture possible of the existing facilities and their conditions. Unfortunately, they cannot be X-rayed, but exploratory investigation is a "must." The older the building, the less chance there is for obtaining existing drawings, and the greater will be the need to investigate the site.

To avoid becoming entangled in a hornet's nest, the merchant should be absolutely certain that the utilities, electrical systems, and structural facilities have been field surveyed. I have seen stores designed with electric feeder lines in existing buildings that were inadequate to meet the new increased requirements.

In one instance, feeder cables had to be run from almost a city block away to achieve the service needed to operate the redesigned store. In another, it was only after the project had been awarded that the merchant discovered two tremendous problems: 1) the existing supply lines were of insufficient size and capacity for his requirements, and 2) the drains were inadequate to accommodate the waste. To correct these unanticipated problems put so great a financial strain on the merchant even before the store was completed that he was never able to recover. This merchant found out the hard way that encountering such conditions after a contract has already been awarded can be disastrous.

Thus it is vital to conduct field investigation of existing facilities in order to evaluate both present needs and costs and alternate solutions. Failing to do so—and starting construction in an existing building without such investigation—is hazardous at best.

CERTIFICATE OF OCCUPANCY

When converting an existing facility that was not previously operated as a retail establishment, it is essential to obtain a license to operate the store. A facility previously operated as a store should also be checked for such a license in order to establish its legality. Too many merchants have spent enormous sums altering space usages, only to discover that they did not have—and could not obtain—the license, called the Certificate of Occupancy, or C.O.

One merchant I know opened a dress shop on the street floor of an apartment building, but failed to verify whether or not he could get a Certificate of Occupancy for the location selected. Only after the store was partially completed did he remember to check into this. Much to his dismay, he discovered that zoning laws prohibited such an establishment, and he was required to close.

Before making any further decisions it is vital to establish whether a C.O. exists or is available. If no C.O. exists but is obtainable, it is also essential to determine who is responsible for obtaining the license, even in new shopping centers. Always remember that the Certificate of Occupancy is the means by which a building is permitted on a given premises.

Chapter 5

Exterior Design Should
Tell a Story

The first thing the public sees when approaching a store is its exterior facade; this is the store's permanent advertisement. As noted in Chapter 1, a properly designed store exterior is informative; it conveys to the customer an impression about the store. Just by looking at the facade, he not only recognizes that this is a retail store, but he can also interpret from the design the caliber and type of merchandise sold within. The entire building concept should communicate whether it is a drug store, a supermarket, a furniture outlet, a couturier shop, or a full-line department store. And it should do so without requiring any intricate thought process on the part of passers-by.

STORE APPROACH AND ENTRANCE

Besides clearly identifying the retail establishment and projecting the quality of merchandise sold within, facade design must also highlight the public access to the store. In addition, the store should be so situated on the site that the vehicular approach is clearly visible and easily accessible. Access routes should not be hidden or confusing. If the predominant stream of customers arriving by automobile must make left-hand turns in the face of heavy on-coming traffic without the benefit of traffic control or a signal light, they will soon become disenchanted with the store.

In planning a store, especially one that is freestanding, the surrounding approaches should not be in conflict; that is, the customer automobile traffic flow should be separated from trucks making deliveries to the stores. And neither automobiles nor trucks should cross the paths of shoppers who are eager to make purchases.

But the fundamental role of a store's exterior design is to appeal—and to appeal specifically to the merchant's chosen customers. If the facade fails to reflect the type and quality of the merchandise it represents, then not only will it attract the wrong shoppers—those who are not interested in the type and quality of the goods in that particular store, but it will also fail to attract those who are. It is as self-defeating for a discount outlet to ape the appearance of a prestige department store as it is for a high style fashion specialty shop to reflect the image of a mass merchandise store.

LOCAL RESTRICTIONS

The store architect, faced with the task of developing the exterior design, must first determine if any restrictions besides building code requirements will be imposed on the design by the community or other outside group. These, where they exist, become the parameters within which he still must accomplish his primary goals of identification and public appeal. When the store is an integral part of a shopping center, the developer is seeking a homogeneous design concept and does not want a crazy quilt pattern of radically different and conflicting store designs; he will want some degree of uniformity in concept within the theme of the shopping center as an entity. Accordingly, there are often restrictive clauses in leases where the landlord reserves the right of approval over the exterior design.

Sometimes, too, the major department store or other anchor stores in the center will have negotiated with the developer the right to approve the designs of neighboring mall and court areas. This often creates something of a tug-of-war here; the department store wants individuality of design to stand out, to be the shining star of the center, while the developer wants all store designs to be integrated so that the entire center appears homogeneous in design concept, so that no one entity is specifically emphasized.

Design integration, however, can be a source of conflict. Many national chains have developed standard designs which reflect the image they wish to present to the public everywhere in the country. When these designs conflict with that of a shopping center, either the chain or the developer must compromise. The direction of the compromise usually depends on whether the chain desires the location more keenly than the developer desires the chain.

The design of both shopping centers and freestanding stores is subject to community restrictions. Just as developers desire conformity with chosen design criteria, so many cities, towns, and neighborhoods require builders to maintain a desired styling. In Washington, for example, there is a Fine Arts Commission which must approve plans and design concepts for new developments. Such bodies have sprung up in towns and cities of all sizes across the country. It's fortunate when the board has members who are professional architects or even lay people of good taste; but it can be disastrous when the approving individuals lack both the appropriate education and background.

Other controlling restrictions involve zoning regulations that limit building heights and sometimes require all buildings to be set back from the street or to harmonize with a selected thematic design. A new Saks Fifth Avenue branch in Frontenac, Mo., for example, received its building permit only on condition that its exterior design be colonial. The reasoning behind this requirement was the community desire to maintain a cohesive town image. Most buildings in the town are of colonial design, including fine, individual homes, and the residents insisted on maintaining a universality of style.

The important point to remember is that not just one agency, but often many must approve the exterior design of the store building. This may include shopping center developers, zoning boards, or fine arts commissions, or the local residents' associations. The merchant and his architect must be aware of any governing restrictions and take them into account at the inception of the design.

This will avoid needless redrawing. "Back to the old drawing board" may seem to be a humorous lament, but it is also a costly one.

SHOW WINDOWS

One element of the facade which warrants careful study is the subject of show windows. In a shopping center, especially an enclosed regional mall, the need for exterior show windows has di-

Figure 5-1 Enclosed windows are fully walled on the sides and back and enclosed on top. The enclosed window has spotlights and flood lights behind the glass. Each window becomes a stage and backdrop for the presentation and dramatization of merchandise. (Saks Fifth Avenue, Hackensack, N.J.)

minished or totally vanished. When the store is located downtown, on Main Street, however, presenting some of the wares in a window display has more significance than it does in a shopping center store. A freestanding building located away from the main pedestrian traffic flow will have a greater need for show windows to attract the attention of its customers.

Windows fall into two basic categories. There are look-through windows and enclosed windows. The enclosed window is fully backed and surrounded by partitions that create a box-like enclosure to display specific wares. (See Figure 5-1.) The look-through window is one that affords a significant view of the store interior, so that both the merchandise within the store and the store itself receive added exposure to passers-by. (See Figure 5-2.) Supermarkets, drug stores, variety, and mass merchandising outlets with interior store displays and dense merchandise inventories on the sales floor are appropriate facilities for the look-through window. So is the fine fashion boutique with its appealing merchandise and interior ambience. Whether a show window is an enclosed or an open look-through is often dictated by the merchandise requirements

Figure 5-2 Look-through windows combine merchandise displays with a view of the store's interior. (Thalhimers, Raleigh, N.C.)

within the store. Enclosed windows provide interior walls that help display the merchandise, which can either be hung on the walls or displayed against them.

In analyzing the desirability of show windows, the merchant should consider the degree to which they contribute to or impede merchandise sales. While a major department store carries multitudinous classifications of merchandise, it has space for only a limited number of show windows. The windows, then, cannot provide for a total merchandise display. Most experienced store buyers will vie for window space when there are ten or more departments for each available window. When a buyer finally succeeds in obtaining a window, he is usually limited by the area to displaying only a fraction of his inventory. Thus the windows cannot really present the full line of merchandise available to customers inside the store; they can only provide a hint.

ENCLOSED SHOW WINDOWS: CONSIDERATIONS

Maintaining show windows is costly. They average from about $8,000 to $12,000 per year per window. If the displays are not kept up-to-date, the windows will fail to meet their primary purpose and intent: the presentation of the newest merchandise.

Besides outright maintenance costs, there are other considerations to keep in mind. You should remember, for example, that the street level is the most productive floor area in the store. When the area devoted to show windows and their access corridors is deducted from the productive sales area, you reduce the sales dollar volume that this area could otherwise earn.

Another consideration is keeping the windows cool. Enclosing a show window creates a build-up of heat due to both the sun and the lighting fixtures. This is what happens in an automobile when it stands in the sunlight with its windows closed. To reduce this heat, the windows must be air-conditioned or ventilated. This adds significantly to the electrical load on the store's systems. Furthermore, if the rays of the sun are not controlled by awnings or tinted glass, merchandise will be damaged by fading as well as by the heat build-up.

Show windows are not without merit, however; they do serve a purpose. But the value of this purpose must be measured carefully to assure that it outweighs all the costs and disadvantages. Where it does not, the merchant is well advised to either minimize the number of show windows or to eliminate them entirely.

ADVANTAGES OF ENCLOSED SHOW WINDOWS

In general, in-city Main Street stores have a greater need for enclosed show windows than those in shopping centers in suburbia. This is because the isolated shopping center creates a captive customer audience. The comparative shopping is limited to the stores and merchandise at the center. Larger, well-known stores will be the first usually visited; the smaller shops generally have a local customer following. The use of windows for merchandise attraction thus becomes secondary.

In cities, however, the competition is much keener. This competition includes not only the other stores on Main Street, but also those on other retail avenues that are within walking distance. Since in-city stores are usually multistoried, making the customer aware of upper-floor merchandise by displaying it in the show windows on street level becomes an important means of drawing their attention.

THE PROS AND CONS OF LOOK-THROUGH WINDOWS

The look-through window also has its pros and cons. Its purpose is to attract and draw customers inside the store both by presenting a view of both the merchandise and the store's ambience. It also creates a desire to enter the store through the power of suggestion: seeing other customers actively shopping inside.

One type of look-through window is a purely visual see-through. It simply offers a view of adjacent departments and of the store interior. Another type features displays in the window through which the public can also see the store interior beyond.

One negative aspect of these windows, however, is that people inside the store see only the reverse side of the displays and the backs of the mannequins that face outside. Another problem is that customers are subjected to the glare of the fixtures required to illuminate the displays. Blinding lights shining into a customer's eyes prohibit his viewing the merchandise.

The use of baffles and screens can eliminate this problem. However, while they avoid the glare, they can also defeat the original purpose of the look-through window, since they block the view of the store's interior. Whenever you plan screen backings, therefore, make sure they are spaced intermittently. This allows them to act as baffles, while they still allow customers a view of the store's interior.

The major drawback of these large glass look-through windows, from a merchandising point of view, however, is that they eliminate valuable wall space from the selling floor. Since walls are places where merchandise can most readily be stocked to greater heights, far more so, generally, than in the middle of the floor, these windows can significantly reduce the merchandise capacity of the store. Furthermore, since walls are a major contributor to the ambience of the store (see Chapter 8), look-through windows also reduce design possibilities.

Large, expansive windows that face the exterior can actually be detrimental to the interior ambience. Sunlight, delivering 5,000 to 10,000 foot-candles or more, streams through the glass and completely eliminates any atmosphere that is designed for 50 or 100 foot-candles. Thus control of sunlight is extremely important when look-through windows are incorporated into a concept. Conversely, when the store is open evenings, there is nothing more uninteresting for customers inside the store than peering through them into darkness. It's obvious, then, that the *indiscriminate* use of windows in store planning must be avoided. Make sure they serve a purpose and that the purpose is worth the cost in terms of money, space loss, and other merchandising uses which must be sacrificed in order to incorporate them into the concept.

THE ENTRANCE

The entrance design should emphasize the location of access to the store. As with the approach to the store, the entrance or entrances should be visible and well defined. The entry should be convenient, properly illuminated for night visibility, and signed, so that the customer is led without question down the path to the entrance. It should leave no question in his mind that this is the customer access.

As for convenience, it must be remembered that some customers are arriving with carriages, some have bundles, some are old, and some are handicapped. An entrance, then, should not only be visible and enhance the facade architecturally, but it also should actively facilitate the flow of customers into and out of the building.

Entrances vary by geographic location. In cold climates, it's necessary to provide vestibules, unless the local code allows for the substitution of revolving doors. A vestibule usually incorporates two sets of doors in an attempt to cut down the draft from the outside. While vestibules provide functional benefits, however, their main drawback is that they take up valuable space. Nevertheless, there are many areas where there simply is no other practical solution.

In designing a vestibule, make sure the two sets of doors are spaced far enough apart so that one customer passing through will not have both doors, inner and outer, open at the same time. A normal separation would be about nine feet so that the customer must take at least two or three steps, giving the first door a chance to close before opening the second one. Closer spacing can defeat the whole purpose of the vestibule.

Some stores have installed air curtains in order to eliminate the need for vestibules. These involve streams of high-velocity conditioned air which resist outside drafts. There are disadvantages to these, however: women can catch their narrow heels in the open floor grills, and the air movement overhead can wreak havoc with hair-dos.

Entrances bring people into the store most effectively when the normal flow of outside pedestrian traffic coincides with the entrance location. They can also either eliminate or contribute to cul-de-sacs or dead areas within the store. If all the customers come in through a single entry, the areas furthest away may have trouble attracting shoppers. But if, for example, there is parking all around the store, then entrances may be spotted at various locations. This helps to eliminate dead areas by encouraging circulation from all sides. On the other hand, built-in security safeguards are necessary, since the same openings that admit customers also are available for shop-lifters to exit through.

SIGNING YOUR STORE

Signs are an important ingredient of exterior design, and although all corporate name signs should identify the store, they vary in function. Large lettered signs are designed to be seen from re-

mote distances. They are aimed at identifying the store and its location for people who drive through the area, even though they are
not necessarily adjacent to the site. The intermediate sized sign identifies one particular store among a group of stores in a shopping
center and is placed to be seen from the surrounding parking areas or
walkways. The smallest signs are those visible only at close range.
Such signs may be plaques in a show window or on the wall adjacent to the entrance.

The first type of sign, the one designed for recognition at a
distance, has large letters faced and sized for maximum exposure.
It is usually either mounted high on the wall of a building or placed
on the top of the building. Such signs should be positioned with
two major considerations in mind: 1) already existing obstructions
to viewers and 2) potential obstructions which may be constructed
at a later date.

These signs should face the direction of the greatest traffic and
population density for maximum awareness. If they are installed
or mounted too high, however, they may not be readable at close
range. If this is the case, intermediate signs may be necessary. However, it is preferable, where possible, to erect a single sign that
can be seen from an optimum distance view and still be easily read
at a closer distance.

When viewers are next to the building, however, no sign of
this type will be readable, especially if the facade is canopied and
if the visibility of the upper section of the facade is obstructed. It
is therefore considered good practice to place smaller signs adjacent to the entrances, in the show windows, or even on the walls at
the corners of the building below the canopy line for adjacent
pedestrians to see.

Whatever type of signs you use, your signing should be an
integral part of the building design. It should not be applied to
the facade as an afterthought. A store's logo and the building architecture should be of one integrated design concept. Whether it has
stylish script or heavy block letters, the signing, like the building,
should identify the corporate name and the type of store it is.

EXTERIOR ILLUMINATION

Outside illumination is applicable to various functions and elements of the facade. If the store is to serve the public at night,
proper lighting of the parking areas and walkways is essential. This

can be accomplished through the use of individual, closely spaced lighting fixtures. These fixtures can be placed relatively low in height and spaced to illuminate a specific, limited area that is within range of the light beam. (See Figure 5-3.) This type of lighting provides an even distribution of illumination and reduces shadows. However, it increases the number of fixtures required and is therefore more costly than the cluster-on-a-pole form of illumination.

Figure 5-3 Individual lighting fixtures provide localized lighting for the immediate area and are used for illuminating limited parking areas, walkways, and planting beds.

Alternatively, clusters of lighting fixtures can be placed on top of high-rise poles, each fixture emitting light in a specific direction. (See Figure 5-4.) While the pole-and-cluster lighting fixtures are not considered as attractive as the individual lighting fixture, they are more economical. This is because using clusters of lights on a common pole requires that only one electric feeder line be run to lighting fixtures that can be aimed in several directions. This reduces the number of poles required, although it varies the intensity of the illumination over the parking area because the poles are further apart.

Even though stores may not be open late at night, a minimal

Figure 5-4   The one, two, and four cluster lighting fixtures shown here are mounted on poles for parking area illumination. In area lighting like this, all the light is directed downward; none is directed upward. This eliminates possible glare or distracting brightness from points of vision above the fixtures, such as from the upper levels of multistory buildings.

intensity of illumination in parking areas is required to reduce the likelihood of crime, drag racing, vandalism, and other antisocial activities during the hours the store is closed. Parking lots, almost by definition, are an attractive nuisance whenever they are not frequented by the general public and when business is not going on.

Finally, the level of illumination should also take into consideration the lighting generated by the show windows. Show window lighting is timed to shut off at a designated hour. Therefore, at least a low level of illumination is required to distinguish vehicles and people.

Signs

Illuminated signing is another feature of nighttime lighting to consider. Both this and parking area illumination must be checked carefully against zoning regulations and building codes. Residences usually surround some of the commercial developments, especially in the suburbs. Because of its disturbing effect, exterior lighting in shopping centers has brought many complaints and even lawsuits, which have resulted in numerous zoning restrictions to control the intensity of outdoor illumination, the size of illuminated signs, the floodlighting of buildings, and even whether such are permitted at all.

Codes usually specify the size of electric signs and restrict the hours of illumination. Naturally, the illuminated sign (like the un-lighted sign) should reflect the quality and the type of store which it identifies. A fine boutique would be out of character blazing with big, block letters that can be seen a mile away. Generally, an il-luminated sign can call proper attention to itself in an area that is relatively dark; attention, after all, is drawn by contrast. If the sur-roundings are ablaze with light while the sign is silhouetted, that contrast can be just as effective as an illuminated sign—and perhaps even more so if it is one more blazing sign among thirty.

Floodlighting

In floodlighting the store, the merchant should analyze care-fully the awareness he seeks to gain, primarily because this type of lighting is quite expensive. It can be costly both to install and to maintain. In fact, the designer must also be careful that it is not an actual detriment to the building. Some floodlights actually empha-size the defects of store construction by casting shadows, which highlight—and even exaggerate—poor and irregular masonry work. While in daylight without shadows, the store may project an attrac-tive and prestigious appearance, nighttime illumination and shad-ows may tend to emphasize poor quality construction.

Of course, floodlighting has its benefits. A freestanding build-ing near a main artery that is heavily trafficked at night can be floodlighted on four sides, or on the front facade only, depending on the advantages to be gained. Or a part of the building can be washed with light. This is a common practice in Europe, where merchants floodlight the upper floors from projecting lower level balconies. If all the neighboring stores use signs to call attention to themselves, another sign might be lost in the forest. So floodlighting is a means of creating store awareness so that the store stands out from the crowd. This can be of particular value if the store facade is architecturally well designed. The store becomes its own sign. Thus, while floodlighting does have advantages, its costs should be studied carefully and balanced against these advantages to determine its merit in each particular situation.

CONSTRUCTION ELEMENTS AND MATERIALS

Of all exterior elements, the basic materials of the store facade and how they are used in its design make the strongest impression on passers-by. However, materials and their application affect building costs significantly. From both standpoints, therefore, extreme care should be exercised in their selection.

The Facade

There are many, many materials available from which to design and construct the facade. These often are related to the styling and design of the exterior. Where the theme must be colonial, for example, the merchant is forced into appropriate building materials such as brick and brick veneers. Where more contemporary designs are formulated, there is a greater freedom of choice among today's modern materials. If these materials are used, they then become themselves a contributing factor in the expression of the architectural design. Of course, materials vary extremely widely in cost, and it is important for the merchant to establish that the price he pays for his chosen material will return its value in appearance, in durability, and in ease of maintenance. (See Figures 5-5 to 5-7.)

Not only do materials vary in composition and cost, but their durability varies with geographical location of the store. Some will resist the rigors of winter, rain, frost, heat, dryness, and other climatic conditions, while others will not. Stucco or cement finishes, for example, stand for years in the South. But in the North, the climatic changes in temperature cause them to expand and to shrink. They develop cracks in which water collects and later freezes, thus enlarging the cracks still further. Eventually, the entire facade may crumble. Similarly, certain marbles, when used in the South, even though subjected to the continued exposure of a hot, bleaching sun and heavy rains, will last much longer than in the North, where the periodic freezing, wide temperature changes, and common cold climate conditions deteriorate them much more quickly.

A material's porosity is also an important factor to consider. Some materials have a greater porosity than others and therefore tend to absorb more dust, dirt, and chemical deposits in the air from nearby factories and vehicular traffic. White marble surfaces and rough textured limestone, for example, tend to stain more readily than other materials, and will therefore require more frequent cleaning.

Another geographic factor in regard to construction materials is their local availability. It is uneconomical to ship basic building materials over very long distances. Therefore, the use of local ma-

Figure 5-5 The material used to create this interesting facade consists of precast panels set in place at the site. This approach tends to reduce construction time in the field. Precast panels can be produced in varied textures, sculptured designs, and colors to fit the design concept. (Diamond's, Phoenix, Ariz.)

terials that are either natural or manufactured in the area where the store is to be built can result in significant savings.

Facades are rarely composed of a homogeneous material. They are constructed with several materials, each providing a different function. One material may provide the general surfacing; another, the trim course; another, the cappings; another, the trims around windows or openings or doors; and still another, the base courses. One material will usually dominate, however, and provide the greatest surface coverage.

Figure 5-6 Exterior materials used on a store's facade need not be limited to masonry. This unusual facade facing is similar to an automobile body: it consists of prefabricated baked enamel metal sections that were assembled at the site. (Ohrbach's, Woodbridge, N.J.)

The selection choices are multitudinous among many different materials, colors, and textures of bricks, clays, ceramic tiles, marbles, glass, granites, fieldstones, and even metals. New products include aluminums and anodized skins. Some are built in place, while others can be prefabricated and brought to the site in sections. Precast, prestressed concrete, for example, has been used for a wide variety of different types of stores. The almost infinite variety of facade material, each playing a different role in store design, provides a wide selection. The designer can therefore base his decisions

Figure 5-7 Stores need not limit their facades to one building material alone; they can use a combination of materials for the design of their facade. This brick facade is combined with precast concrete sun screen and trim to provide a functional and harmonious design concept. (Diamond's, Tucson, Ariz.)

on the availability and cost of the product, on its contribution to the exterior ambience of the store, and on the cost of construction, installation, and maintenance.

One word of caution in using several different materials: too many will give the facade a patchwork quilt appearance. Limiting the number of different surface materials will simplify the facade design.

Exterior Walls

Walls have another function besides enclosing the space within; they also serve to contain and insulate the conditioned inside area. Many materials have built-in insulating properties; others do not and require that insulating material be incorporated into the wall construction. In this era of constantly increasing costs for electricity and heating fuels, very significant savings in store operating costs can be realized through often minor expenditures on insulation.

Such insulation can serve to reduce the building's heat gain from the outside in the summer, thus relieving the load on the air conditioning system. And it can hold heat within the store in winter, reducing the consumption of heating fuel. Thus, besides improving the store's operating costs, insulation can also increase the comfort of customers and employees alike.

In enclosed shopping center malls, except for the major anchors, stores have little or no control over the design of those walls that are exposed to the exterior. Since this outside wall—the wall exposed to the weather and the elements—is common to all mall shops, the design must relate to the overall concept, not to an individual store. Stores do, however, within any limitations imposed by their leases, have control over the interior surfacing and treatment of these walls, as well as over the store fronts facing the inside of the mall, subject to the developer's approval.

STORES IN ENCLOSED MALLS

There is a tremendous difference between being located in an enclosed mall and being located either on Main Street or in an open shopping center. One reason for this difference is weather conditions. Inside the enclosed mall, store facades need not be constructed of materials designed to withstand the elements of weather, since they are protected by a climatized mall.

Another reason, however, is based on the concept behind the enclosed mall. In these malls individual shops are part of a total concept. As such, they neither desire nor require enclosed fronts to separate them from the common mall. In fact, the enclosed mall concept is based on open front facades that offer customers the freedom to circulate from the mall into each and every store without physical restriction, much as they would walk from one department to another in a major department store. Thus one effect of an enclosed shopping center mall is to eliminate the barrier which may psychologically keep a customer from entering a shop.

When designing an open store front, the store architect has to overcome some unique problems. For example, the merchant must be able to close up at night. With an open facade, the conventional door will not serve the purpose. What is more, since many malls are pedestrian arcades when the stores are closed, most merchants want to achieve advertising value from the goods on display during closing hours. Thus some of the enclosures are glass, while others are a sliding metal grille that allows customers to view both the store interior and the merchandise on display. The grillwork in enclosed malls, however, are far more decorative than those installed purely for security reasons.

The design of such store fronts, based on minimal facade surface materials, is also a challenge to the architect. He must provide public awareness and store identity, differentiating the store from its neighbors through the design of a store front which has minimal frontal surface for conceptual development, and within the limitations imposed by the developer. Generally, the shop itself, with its merchandise on display, is a strong contributing element to its own identity.

Show windows that enclose the store fronts are seldom used in an enclosed mall. This is because the majority of shops are planned to provide an entire or partial frontage for both merchandise display and customer browsing. Most shops, of course, do provide some type of display, either enclosed or open, at the store's mall line. And a few, tied perhaps to traditions which originated long before enclosed malls ever existed, still erect a facade that recalls the Main Street facade, but which still incorporates the concept of the open front. Stores with expansive fronts, however, rarely devote their entire store front to the open concept, since it would reduce the capacity of merchandise housed against the wall. Thus many of these stores include walls in their store front concepts, but the walls are usually minimal in length.

Chapter 6

Interior Space Allocation

Even before many of the decisions have been made affecting the building shell of the store and its exterior design, the merchant and his architect must resolve many basic elements of the store's interior layout. To describe the general principles involved in this area of store planning, this chapter will deal with the full-line department store. The fundamental problems that must be overcome for this type of outlet are similar to those affecting a large chain store which anchors a regional shopping center, and the principles apply within budgetary limitations to mass merchandise, variety, discount, and drug stores where size and ambience are apt to be the greatest areas of difference. More specialized retailers still require certain primary store functions included in a department store, and their merchandise classifications can be treated as a coordinated group of departments in a larger unit.

SPACE APPORTIONMENT

The Building Function

Given the shape and gross area of the store, the first step is to apportion them among three functional areas: the space needed for building functions, nonselling services, and the sales area. In terms of space requirements, building functions, depending on store size and code requirements, are generally constant, except where a highly specialized operation calls for more equipment rooms than normal; the main variable in building function area is between single and multilevel units. With more than one level, the space devoted to stairs, elevators, escalators, pipe shafts, duct runs, and weight-bearing structural elements materially increases the bite taken by this nonusable area. Usually, building functions occupy 7% to 10% of the gross area for branch department stores and may go as high as 20% or more in center-city, highrise flagship units.

The location of some building functions such as exterior walls is predetermined; for others it can be more flexible. In a single level store, the area occupied by building functions may not have any major affect on the remaining net usable area. However, they must be located carefully to assure the store's operational efficiency. In a multilevel unit, the overall usable space may stay the same regardless of the location of building functions, but on the individual levels the space will vary, depending on where these functions are placed. The relationship to selling of such building functions as entrances, escalators, and elevators has been discussed to some extent in Chapters 3 and 5. The location of merchandise departments and how they are affected by these functions, however, must be considered.

The placement of equipment rooms, for example, can affect the cost as well as the usable space surrounding them. If outside electric or plumbing lines enter the store on one side, it is seldom practical to run main feeder and supply lines to equipment rooms on the opposite wall. At the same time, these rooms should be located for the most economical serving of the store as a whole, and where internal runs of lines will be minimized. Placing equipment rooms on upper levels also increases the cost of running main feeders from below the street entry of utility services and usually requires structural reinforcement. The merchant must weigh both the loss of space occupied by these and other building functions and their cost against the possible elimination of valuable space which might be used as productive selling area. There are circumstances when the one-time cost for a remotely located equipment room can be offset by the continuing benefits of sales volumes gained through the relocation of this building function from prime sales area.

Stairs, of course, must meet fire code requirements. But there is usually some flexibility in their location within the code. In fact, there is no great cost penalty or space loss between varied locations. They should, then, be placed within the code, where they will do the most good and the least damage to the overall merchandise plan, present and future. (Sprinklers and other mechanical equipment are covered in detail in Chapter 11.)

Nonselling Services

In the usable area left to the store planner after building function areas are subtracted, the proper balance between selling and nonselling functions is widely variable and depends on many influencing factors. The goal is to obtain maximum selling area, since this is the primary objective of the entire building. But this goal must be achieved without limiting nonselling services to a point where they either create bottlenecks or handicap the sales functions. Receiving facilities, for example, must be large enough to accommodate an incoming flow of merchandise adequate to keep the store fully stocked. But they must be located removed from customer entrances so that truck traffic doesn't interfere with the flow of customer traffic.

The amount of space devoted to stockrooms will depend on the amount of backup merchandise needed beyond the stock carried on the sales floor. The amount of merchandise warehoused within the store itself, in turn, will depend on the frequency of deliveries with which the store can be served by a distribution center or from a larger store in its locality. Or the store may itself serve smaller units nearby. If the store will receive shipments directly from manufacturers, space must be devoted to facilities for price-marking and tagging merchandise. In-store merchandise alterations will require space, as will credit facilities and general offices if included in the operation. Some manufacturers also ticket and warehouse for stores.

The list of the various store functions on pp. 20 and 21 includes most of the nonselling operations. These must be checked carefully to see that adequate space is allotted for the store's maximum efficiency. Typical space requirements for many of these functions (excluding credit and general offices) are shown in Figure 6-1. Depending on the facilities needed to support the selling functions, nonselling areas can vary from 8% to 15% of a store's gross

Figure 6-1 The following is a typical breakdown developed for a store of 110,000 square feet. This example presents a conventional store whose

---

FIRST FLOOR

Gross Area of Floor	55,000 S/F (100%)
Building Functions	4,225 S/F (8%)
Nonselling Areas	5,175 S/F (9%)
Available Selling Area	45,600 S/F (83%)

BUILDING FUNCTIONS

Exterior Walls	1100 S/F
Stairs	1160
Escalators	280
Passenger Elevator	65
Freight Elevator	125
Elevator Machine Room	210
Electric Closets	100
Electric Service Room	330
Incinerator Room	455
Water, Gas & Meter Room	260
Janitor Closet	60
Pump Room	80
	4225 S/F

NONSELLING

Truck Dock	1115 S/F
Floor Receiving	385
Security	115
Parcel Check	220
Alteration Room	635
Show Windows	195
Circulation	810
Trucking Corridor	1050
Vestibule	350
Service Desk	300
	5175 S/F

SELLING AREA (Planned)

Departments	Area	Fitting Rooms	Stock	Total
Foundations	1700	170	300	2,170 S/F
Daytime Dresses	2775	210	225	3,210
Lingerie (Intimate)	2275		400	2,675
Dresses	4100	610	220	4,930
Coats & Suits	2855			2,855
Sportswear	3920	420	340	4,680
Candy	340		325	665
Promotion	750			750
Millinery & Wigs	550			550
Hosiery	1075			1,075
Handbags-Small Leather Goods	1800			1,800
Neckwear-Handkerchiefs	1045			1,045
Jewelry	650			650
Juniors	4160	365	250	4,775
Women's Shoes	1750		1740	3,490
Cosmetics	2600		60	2,660
Men's Furnishings	2800			2,800
Men's Clothing	2650	175	900	3,725
Men's Shoes	220		200	420
Accessories			245	245
Stationery	430			430
				45,600 S/F

operation provides for receiving of partial shipments from manufacturers with credit and general office functions being performed from a remote central flagship or parent store.

SECOND FLOOR

Gross Area of Floor	55,000 S/F (100%)	
Building Functions	7,125 S/F (13%)	
Nonselling Areas	11,940 S/F (22%)	
Available Selling Area	35,935 S/F (65%)	

BUILDING FUNCTIONS

Exterior Walls	1100 S/F
Stairs	990
Escalators	360
Passenger Elevator	65
Freight Elevator	125
Electrical Closet	225
Boiler Room	1460
H.V.A.C. Room (1)	1440
H.V.A.C. Room (2)	1360
	7125 S/F

NONSELLING

Key Rec.	300 S/F
Display & Sign Writer	640
Gift Wrap-Shipping	525
Employees' Facilities	1,900
Employees' Canteen	900
Maintenance Shop	235
Circulation	100
Receiving & Marking	4,650
Public Toilets & Offices	2,690
	11,940 S/F

SELLING AREA (Planned)

Departments	Area	Fitting Rooms	Stock	Total
Housewares	5000		1800	6,800 S/F
Bath Shop	600			600
Domestics & Pillows	4700		590	5,290
Curtains & Draperies	4520		1500	6,020
China & Glassware	2600		1000	3,600
Girls 7–14	1830			
Girls 3–6	1115	125	520	4,500
Teens	910			
Children's Shoes	420		280	700
Infants & Layette	1705		670	2,375
Toddlers	915			915
Accessories & Underwear	700			700
Boys 8–20	2170			
		50	600	3,650
Boys 4–7	830			
Luggage	785			785
				35,935 S/F

RECAP OF AREAS

Levels	Building Functions	Nonselling Areas	Selling Areas	Total
First Floor	4,225 S/F	5,175 S/F	45,600 S/F	55,000 S/F
Second Floor	7,125 S/F	11,940 S/F	35,935 S/F	55,000 S/F
Totals	11,350 S/F	17,115 S/F	81,535 S/F	110,000 S/F
	(10.32%)	(15.56%)	(74.12%)	(100%)

area. Also deducting 7% to 10% for building functions (or even 20% in a highrise flagship), this leaves between 65% and 85% available for sales. Most branch stores average between 70% and 85% for selling area.

The Sales Floor

Before establishing a breakdown of the selling area, the merchant should do a self-analysis and evaluation. Where does his marketing strength lie? Is he known for his fashions, accessories, or home furnishings? Hard lines or soft lines? White goods, such as refrigerators, or brown goods, such as furniture? Does his reputation favor men's, women's, children's, or family apparel? Or is he best known for glass, china, gifts, and linens?

The answers to these questions will have a direct relationship to the space assigned to each department. Yet the merchant must also be careful not to devote too much space for one favored merchandise classification at the expense of other departments whose insufficient area for depth of stock might unbalance the store and create a merchandising weakness. Generally speaking, when a department is unable to carry sufficient styles, sizes, colors, or price ranges because of limited space, it is better to omit the classification entirely, rather than to provide scant representation. Insufficient depth of stock in one department conveys to the customer an image of inadequacy for the entire store.

If the store is to be a unit of a chain or an additional store for corporation with multiple branch stores, in-house statistics will be available for evaluating successful departments in terms of area, linear feet of fixture required, necessary stock and fitting rooms, and department location within the store. Errors made by unsuccessful departments are also valuable measuring sticks which can be used to make corrective decisions in the planning of the new store. Oversize, undersize, and unprofitable operations in existing units are readily detectable, but evaluations must consider the market contexts in which they exist, including customer income, population density, family characteristics, and competition. Where no other stores or in-house statistics are available, industry averages are published by such outside sources as the National Retail Merchants

Association. These figures can also be used as checks against whatever in-house statistics may exist.

DETERMINING REQUIRED SPACE

Besides the total store size, anticipated dollar volume is also a required determinant for department sizing (see Chapter 2). There is a direct relationship between a department's sales volume and the space allotted to it. Suppose, for example, that a merchant wishes to determine the size of a dress department. Based on his initial investigation and analysis, he anticipates a total store volume of $7,000,000 annually from a sales area of 82,500 square feet. Both his past experience and statistics show that 5% of the total store volume, or $350,000, is a reasonable goal for a classification of dresses. Since his average dress sale amounts to $17.50 per item, he will have to sell 20,000 dresses during the year to meet his goal. After determining that he averages three complete stock turnovers per year in this merchandise classification, he finds that he must maintain in this store an average unit stock of approximately 6,667 dresses.

The merchandise fixtures being considered for dress presentation will accommodate ten dresses per linear foot, and including its prorated half of the adjoining aisle requires a floor depth of six feet for both the fixture depth and half of the adjacent aisle. Thus ten dresses will require six square feet of sales area, and the entire stock of 6,667 dresses will require approximately 4,000 square feet. Adding the fitting room, adjacent stock area, wrapping, and display requirements which may range from 800 to 900 square feet, he arrives at a total department size of 4,800 to 4,900 square feet.

A quicker method for determining department size is simply to divide the projected annual dollar volume by the statistical dollar sales per square foot, but the merchant must be careful to apply the *appropriate* figures. As in the above example, an anticipated annual store volume of $7,000,000, containing a sales area of 82,500 square feet provides a *total* store average of just under $85 per square foot.

But total averages are often misleading. If the overall store average is applied to determine the area allotment for dresses, dividing the $350,000 anticipated dress volume by $85 would result in a department size of only a little more than 4,100 square feet—

some 700 square feet less than would be needed to accommodate the inventory, fitting rooms, and adjacent stock required to reach the projected volume.

In fact, departments differ drastically in the amount of space needed to do a given dollar volume. Some merchandise which is both high in unit sales and compact in size delivers far above the store average dollar volume per square foot it occupies; other classifications require more space for stock and display and deliver less volume per square foot. The merchant in the example above could rather have checked his experience and statistics from other stores

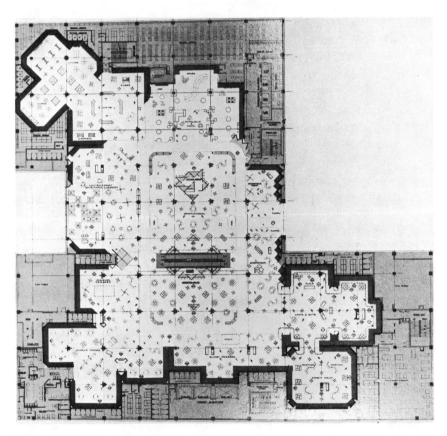

Figure 6-2 This open concept plan has a few shops that are enclosed around the perimeter. The central area and surrounding merchandise groupings have no high wall obstructions or partitions. Generally, the partitions encompass only a section of a department and are used mostly as background. This arrangement provides an unobstructed view of the floor's sales area.

and found that his *dress departments* in similar markets produced an average of $73 per square foot. By dividing his projected department volume of $350,000 by $73, a department size of 4,800 results—and basically agrees with the more detailed method of approach.

THREE BASIC STORE PLANS

In formulating the interior layout of a new store, the overall concept for the selling area is planned in accordance with the statistical analysis of departments. There are three basic concepts for store planning: *the open plan, the enclosed* (or *shop* or *boutique*) *plan,* and *the zone and cluster plan.*

The Open Plan

Open plans provide for a complete open sales space surrounded by perimeter walls. (See Figure 6-2.) All subdivisions for departmental definitions and all fixtures are usually kept below eye level or are made porous in design to permit visibility throughout the sales floor. Most low end merchandise stores, discount, variety, and drug stores use the open plan concept. It provides better staff interselling and surveillance as well as better visibility for all departments on the floor.

Its main drawback, however, is that while it enhances staff coverage, security, and exposure of merchandise, it reduces the opportunity for a complete separation of merchandise classifications, where each group of merchandise has its own home and independent ambience. The lack of physical separation generally contributes to the conflict of having unrelated merchandise rub shoulders.

The Enclosed Plan

The enclosed plan has been extremely popular in the past. This approach subdivides merchandise classifications so that each merchandise category has its own "shop" within the store, and each has its own identity, style, color, and ambience. (See Figure 6-3.) Arising from the success of the specialty stores using "boutique" design techniques largely borrowed from Europe, this plan usually

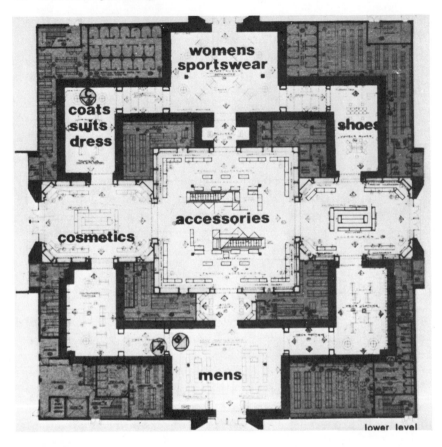

Figure 6-3 This layout shows an enclosed concept plan. Each merchandise classification is located within an enclosed area that is surrounded by high walls. All shops are interconnected through walkways that surround the central area and provide access to it.

results in higher construction costs when adapted as a concept in a full-line department store (as opposed to lower costs in specialty store of limited size). It requires wall separations between shops, which in turn call for more individual shop staffing, greater security safeguards (because of the lack of visibility), and more supervision of staff and customers than would normally have to be allotted to an open plan concept. Furthermore, flexibility is limited and future changes are costly, due to the need for structural remodeling. The concept has, however, been particularly successful in merchandising for the more prestigious commercial establishments, where higher priced merchandise lines can support the additional overhead costs.

The Zone and Cluster Plan

The need by many stores to keep the cost of operations down, to provide a degree of flexibility, to maintain security, and still to provide some definition between departments as well as a varied am-

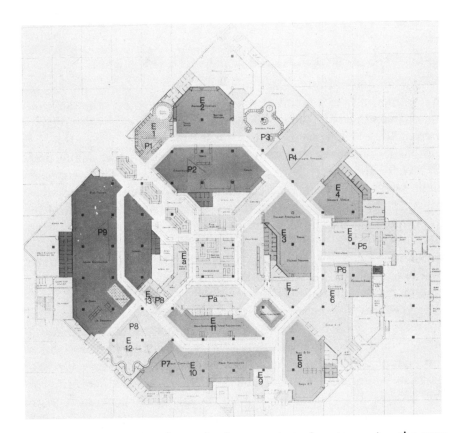

Figure 6-4   This plan shows the floor concept of a store using the zone and cluster plan. Each department that specializes in a category of merchandise is zoned around a central area. Within each zone the related classifications of merchandise are clustered to create a particular merchandise world.

bience has led to the increasing popularity of the zone and cluster plan. This incorporates the best features of the other two concepts (see Figure 6-4). The sales floor is divided into large areas of associated merchandise groups, rather than into small, individually merchandised boutiques. High wall dividers or high-rise fixtures separate the zones, providing completely integrated worlds of related merchandise. The departments within the zones are divided by mobile and relatively transparent clusters of fixtures. Each zone contains flexibility and allows for security, cross-coverage by the sales staff, and supervision. The zone and cluster plan permits a change of styling, design, and ambience in each zone as if a series of large specialty stores with associated merchandise were placed next to each other.

GROUPING AND LOCATING DEPARTMENTS

After determining which planning concept you want to use and estimating the amount of space you will devote to the different merchandise classifications, the next steps are to group the related merchandise departments and to locate them within the store. In the past, stores have grouped merchandise within the selling area largely for the convenience of the store's own staff. This was especially true where several classifications were purchased by one store buyer. The reasoning was that direct, all-inclusive visual control by the responsible executive was the answer to proper merchandising. At times, the responsibilities of a single buyer covered groups of goods that had no relationship to each other, except perhaps the source of supply. Yet the classifications were offered for sale in adjoining locations only to help the buyer keep tabs on it.

As stores began to realize that the customer, rather than the buyer, is the one who must be served, an upheaval took place in the arrangement of merchandize on the sales floor. Leading stores throughout the United States began to coordinate merchandise displays in conformity with customers' buying habits, discovering in the process that convenience for the customer generated more sales.

Merchandise Geared to Buying Patterns

Formerly, one staff buyer of the store would select tablecloths, napkins, sheets, pillow cases, and towels, which were all grouped together in one linen department. Today, however, varied merchandise is separated and aligned with other coordinated and related goods, all based on the customer's use. Thus tablecloths and napkins are placed with their rightful partners, dishes, glasses, tableware, artificial flowers—all items normally found on the dining room table.

Presentation of related merchandise in one area coordinates the customer's shopping and leads to reciprocal sales. Towels coordinate better with bathroom accessories such as shower curtains, bath mats, and soap dishes than it does with table linen. Similarly, sheets and pillow cases relate best to blankets, pillows, and mattresses.

Today's customers also are oriented toward buying fashion merchandise by coordination: gloves with handbags, handbags with shoes, blouses with skirts and slacks, ties with shirts, and even sportswear with sporting goods. Placing two or more coordinated merchandise classifications close together to conform with the customer's buying habits generates sales that might not materialize if the related goods were remote from one another.

By placing all classifications related to one merchandise category together in one area, as in the zone and cluster plan, or all on one floor, the planner creates "merchandise worlds," such as a "fashion world" or a "home furnishings world." The same approach can even be extended to incorporate utility merchandise such as hardware, auto supplies, do-it-yourself materials, and garden equipment.

Merchandise Classifications within the Store

Locating the groups of merchandise classifications within the store is simpler in a single-level building than in a multilevel store. Departments are either up front, centered toward the rear, or at the sides.

Moreover, the same principles that apply to the position of one department among many also apply to site selection for one specialized store among many. In Chapter 2 we described how a tobacco shop would require an especially convenient site since customers will not travel longer distances than absolutely necessary for a lipstick or other frequently sold, fast turnover merchandise. Furniture shoppers, on the other hand, are apt to expend both time and thought on their major purchases and thus are willing to go to greater distances in order to make a selection. Thus the cosmetic department would be best located adjacent to or very near a trafficked entrance. The furniture department, on the other hand, can be located in a remote area, even on the top floor of a multilevel unit or in a rear corner of a single level unit.

It should be pointed out that the furniture outlet, which needs a much larger display area, will not want to locate in the highest rent district. Stores, much like departments in a store, apply similar reasoning in positioning their locations.

LOCATION AFFECTS MERCHANDISING EFFECTIVENESS

The store planner should consider his store interior as being comprised of real estate locations of varied value. In multistory buildings where the customer enters on the street level only, the first floor naturally has the greatest amount of traffic, since everyone entering the store must pass through this level. Almost always, then, the entrance level produces the largest dollar volume and income, sometimes averaging two or three times that of any other floor.

The importance of floors usually diminishes in proportion to their distance from the main floor. The variable between the second and third floor, while significant, may be relatively small; the aggregate difference between a second and a sixth floor, however, can be considerable.

On each sales floor there are important "100% locations"—areas most heavily trafficked—where customers tend to congregate. These include areas around entrances, escalators, and elevators. Even the space around entrances varies in merchandising strength, according to the number of customers using the entrance. Where a department reflects particular merchandising strength, including productivity and profitability, it is a candidate for a 100% location, assuming that 1) it can be housed properly and conveniently, and 2) it has no physical requirements that will displace another equally or more important classification. Fast turnover is not the only consideration here; high volume and profitability are also necessary to support the high value of the space occupied.

Indeed, many stores literally charge varying "rents" to each department in relation to the value of their locations and size. Floor space adjacent to entrances carries a much higher charge per square foot than the same location on the floors above or below.

Similarly, space surrounding entrances and escalators is more valuable than space in a remote corner. The sum total of departmental rents will equal the store's total cost of occupying the building, of course, but the burden on each department depends on the merchandising effectiveness of its location.

USING ELEVATORS VS. ESCALATORS

When elevators are used to transport customers to and from the selling floors, customer exposure to merchandise decreases. Little if any merchandise is visible to those riding the elevator. However, elevators are particularly important for transportation to the upper floors, since slower means of ascent can discourage customers from visiting departments there. Once a customer enters an elevator car, his travel time is almost negligible.

Escalators, on the other hand, slow the customer down. They require him to move from one run to another on each floor he ascends or descends. This slows down and enforces movement around the escalator well on each floor, thus increasing the value of the space around the well by creating merchandise exposure, especially on the lower levels. The adjacent locations are excellent spots for high turnover, promotional, or sale merchandise. Customers descending on the escalator are usually exposed to wide areas of the sales floor they are approaching and to a broad selection of merchandise.

Escalators also provide a slow ascent to the upper floors of a multistoried building, moving large numbers of customers up and down. Merchandise displays on each of these levels help to keep the customer engrossed as he or she ascends or descends. By far the most popular means of customer transportation between floors, escalators are particularly valuable for the visibility they offer the floor and adjacent merchandise.

DEPARTMENTS ON THE UPPER AND LOWER FLOORS

With the diminishing importance of space on the higher levels, the store planner should place departments with greater area demand and higher unit sales, such as furniture, in these remote location to the same degree as other departments which depend on high frequency turnover.

In addition, locating the various nonselling functions on the upper levels wherever practical allows them to occupy a less valuable space, freeing more productive areas for selling space. Should some of these functions provide customer services, such as a credit department, they will draw customer traffic up to these floors through the sales areas. Since customer circulation is the store's life blood and must flow through the store to keep it alive, many merchants purposely place customer services or even restaurants on the upper floors to attract traffic.

Basement selling areas, due to their proximity to the street or main floor, are extremely important. The psychological aspects of this location, however, must be considered. The "bargain basement" promotional approach so common in department stores for many years has rubbed off on the goods displayed there, and customers tend to rebel against purchasing prestige merchandise in basement levels. In spite of this, however, below-grade floors are known to be high-volume areas. In addition to bargain merchandise, other classifications are being located here with more and more success. These include utility goods, home furnishings, furniture, gifts, glassware, china, floor coverings, toys, sporting goods, major appliances, leisure merchandise, and even eating facilities.

THE OVERALL PLAN: AIM FOR FLEXIBILITY

Having decided each department's allotment of the space and its general location within the store, the planner is next faced with fitting the pieces of the overall jigsaw puzzle into the actual store building. Here is where the decision regarding the building's bay size becomes so important. The bays, or spaces between weight-supporting columns and the limiting periphery walls, define the areas in which he has to develop his concept. Within this area, he plans his layout and adapts a spacing of elements that will, as far as possible, provide a standard space modulation which ties together the individual department components, fixtures, partitions, and the building services such as lighting, air conditioning, and sprinklers. The planner fits the *grid*, or repetitious pattern, into the department configuration. Through the utilization of standard components and spacing, the grid facilitates flexibility for the future.

Styles are always changing. Changes create various fixturization demands on shops and stores to meet new merchandise requirements. To keep up with this kaleidoscopic condition, a store must be flexible, and flexibility of store interiors is an integral part of modern store planning. Of course, flexibility can vary greatly in degree; it can amount to seasonally changing a shelf for a hangrod or to merely adding or removing a few store fixtures. It can consist of enlarging or shrinking a merchandise classification within a department, expanding or contracting the full department, or even to physically enlarging the entire store.

The degree to which flexibility can be built in has not always been clearly understood by merchants. In order to meet every contingency, some owners of larger stores, especially, have insisted on an exaggerated amount of built-in flexibility. Since this is not cost free—in fact, it can be extremely expensive—the costs of opening these stores were unnecessarily high. Unused built-in flexibility that fails to gain any merchandising advantage is a noncontributing cost that affects the profitability of the store.

Wholesale unevaluated incorporation of flexibility can be as damaging as neglecting this vital characteristic. There must be a preplanned purpose and careful design consideration for all flexible elements included in the store, from modulated ceiling/lighting systems to take-apart store fixtures. If it is not handled correctly, the result can look like a model put together with a child's tinker toy set, rather than a store designed and constructed by professionals. Evaluation of the store's degree of flexibility should be based on the present and anticipated future use of all facilities, taking into account past experience and related costs.

Chapter 7

Store Fixtures

If a store is a machine for selling goods—and it is—then the parts of the machine that are most functional are the store fixtures, since they hold and display the merchandise to be sold. Fixturing is the one aspect of store planning and design that is unique to retail architecture and construction. Indeed, some individual fixtures are unique to specific types of stores and even to certain quality merchandise. In self-service stores, they must perform almost all of the functions of a sales clerk except that of receiving the money for the purchase. (If a vending machine is considered a store fixture, even that function is filled.) In stores where a sales staff provides greater degrees of customer assistance, fixtures should aid the staff by presenting merchandise in the most attractive and enticing fashion possible.

NEW FIXTURE CHANGES AND DEVELOPMENTS

Regardless of the quality and type of store, however, fixtures today are undergoing major changes. The tiered, shelved, or single-level table, gondola, or garment rack grouped in seemingly endless straight runs, is being replaced by more imaginative fixtures designed to create interest at point of sale for specific merchandise classifications. Since the cost of both fixtures and of space on the sales floor have skyrocketed, fixtures are being designed to increase the capacity and productivity of each square foot to display and sell merchandise. Merchants have recognized that high construction costs are not always compatible with low-level displays and merchandise presentations that utilize only four or five feet of the height available to them. The entire cubic content of the space, not simply the square footage, must be used to maximum advantage.

Certainly all fixtures cannot rise like trees in a forest so that they obscure the visibility of merchandise and, in most cases, defeat their own purpose. Recently, modular, adjustable fixture systems have been developed that can be placed on the sales floor so as to take advantage of intermittent cubical spaces and to create varied interest throughout the store. By breaking the monotonous runs of standard fixture heights, these techniques permit the highlighting of departments as boutiques or shops on the floor, which would have been lost in a sea of tables and gondolas in the past.

Another change is the replacement of costly fixture assemblies. Instead of assembling multiple parts with nails or screws or glue, premolded forms are being adapted. Plastic and other composition materials allow the one-piece molding of drawers and chassis, thus eliminating the costly and tedious work of assembly. What's more, transparent elements such as glass and clear plastic have been strengthened, so that instead of requiring support themselves, as in the past, they can now support the rods, shelves, and bins that contain the merchandise. As they replace the wooden or metal rack ends of yesteryear, the goods on display become more and more visible to more and more shoppers.

Finally, fixture systems of hardware and standardization of modulated component parts permit the interchange of shelves, rods, drawers, bins, and even complete fixtures throughout a store. Through the use of these systems, fixture modules can be moved from one wall to another or even out onto the middle of the sales area, providing maximum flexibility—and all without the need for skilled craft labor. Clearly, this reduces the cost of fixture relocation, promotes adaptability, and at the same time improves the opportunities of meeting merchandise demands. What's more, in spite of the multiplicity of functions, these modular fixture systems still harmonize with the total store and department ambience.

THE PLANNING TEAM

Merchandise fixture selections are an integral part of the store planning process. As explained in Chapter 6, specific department sizes and configurations must provide for a specific amount of merchandise to be carried on the sales floor. This in turn depends on the merchandise capacity of the fixtures to be used.

But decisions regarding fixtures are not a one-man consideration. Despite the store planner's presumed expertise and assignment of fitting the departments into the space available, fixtures have other characteristics besides providing a merchandise capacity and presentation. The proper choice requires that a method of presentation be considered. Whether the garment will be hung or folded, binned or shelved is a decision of store policy. It is a job for a team, especially in major stores of magnitude, where fixture selection involves a tremendous amount of work.

The fixture team should be neither too large nor too small; while one man is not enough, eight are too many. Let function be the guide. The merchant's own store planning director, of course, belongs on the team, which should be spearheaded by the outside architectural, planning, and design consultant. The consultant is responsible for the assessment of the fixtures' technical and construction aspects, including material selection, as well as of their integration with the other physical and design elements of the store. There should also be a store operations executive on the team. Not only do fixtures require maintenance, but many incorporate lighting, mechanical, and security elements, which all affect general store operations. Finally, from time to time the display director should also be brought into the planning meetings for his participation and advice. The top executive should also be on the team, as well as the store's senior merchandiser.

No other single component of the store is more directly related to the primary purpose of selling goods than the fixturing. Especially when multiple methods of merchandise presentations are adaptable within the framework of today's fixture concepts. The leadership and

WHAT IS THE FUNCTION OF THE STORE ARCHITECT/DESIGNER?

An architect should:

- assist the client to properly evaluate his needs and desires
- reflect the client's needs graphically into documents for construction
- technically fulfill the client's needs and requirements within the framework of good planning and design
- Convince the client to reevaluate pitfalls and solve potential problems before they arise
- maintain the store's philosophy wherever possible

An architect should *not:*

- be responsible to set the store merchandising philosophies
- be responsible for the store's success
- plan and design his project as a product of his own efforts and imagination alone
- carry out the client's wishes without criticism, even if he sees potential problems or errors
- refuse to solve the client's demands when he disagrees with them but cannot convince the client otherwise

final decision-making authority of a top executive is necessary to set store policy and to keep the varied requirements of individual departments from overcomplicating the system or even working at cross-purpose with its primary aims of fixturization.

All of these people must be responsible for assuring that all aspects have been considered, and that the final selection is, indeed, final. Perhaps the greatest waste of time, effort, and money in new store construction and alterations results from changes in previously made fixture plans and design decisions. Store executives are notorious for this. The later the change, the greater the additional expense and loss. Early changes, which may require only drafting alterations, are less costly, but even these result in critical time losses.

Not only does a change require additional expenditures, but its tentacles are far-reaching and affect other areas. It may hold up electrical work or alter the mechanical system. A simple color change will affect coordinated decorative accessories such as floor coverings or uphostery materials. In fact, last-minute fixture changes have even caused late store openings, and the loss of significant dollar volumes as a result, due to purchasing seasonal merchandise that was outmoded by the late opening.

Procrastination in decision-making is equally responsible for causing late openings and carries comparable penalties. The architect, designer, and store planner must impress these facts on the other members of the team. There must be a realistic schedule which includes a date of approval, and everyone must adhere to this schedule to assure that the store opens on time with a minimum of extra expense.

MERCHANDISE PRESENTATION TECHNIQUES

In the selection and design of fixtures, it is also important to evaluate merchandise presentation techniques. Will the goods be shelved, hung, or put in bins? For hangware, will the shoulders show or will the face of the garment be presented in waterfall fashion? Will the fixture be binned or will it have dividers? Will the shelves and rods be adjustable? What about lighting? Will the merchandise be illuminated from the fixture itself or from the ceiling? Will the fixture highlight the merchandise it carries or will it also identify the department? How will its height affect the visibility of other areas of the store? Will the materials of which it is built blend with the other elements of the department and still perform their function? Should it be portable or adjustable by regular store personnel?

Fixture functions vary from one type of retail operation to another and depend upon management preference, but all have the common goal of helping to sell the greatest amount of merchandise possible in a given amount of space within budgeted cost while conforming to the chosen atmosphere of the store.

"Within budgeted cost": easy to say, but difficult to achieve. Both inflation and recent concepts of merchandising have contributed to the skyrocketing fixture prices currently prevalent. Cutting up interiors into individual shops and boutiques, for example, can require walls which can cost as much as four times those used in the open plan store of yesterday. While store planners cannot blink away the increases due to inflation, they can and should work to minimize costs through in-depth analysis and evaluation of each and every facet of fixture construction and composition.

They should particularly question outmoded design and costly construction standards which were established in the past, not only when prices were lower, but when store expansion almost automatically provided ever-increasing dollar volumes and profits. Those days are gone, and their standards no longer apply. Repeating these standards, although the easy way out, is a costly and possibly fatal procedure during times of high costs combined with a tight economy. Unfortunately, few fields of endeavor cling so tenaciously to past practices and successes as does retailing. The very businessmen who recognize and even anticipate radical changes in customer preferences for merchandise find it most difficult to see the need for change in their own practices and operations. Although merchandise capacities are important, overstocking, when it violates a dramatic presentation, should be avoided.

PERFORM COST ANALYSES

Of course, successful fixture design considerations should not be abandoned out of hand. Rather, they should be discriminately appraised to assure that their functional value is in line with their increased cost. Many times, the elimination or substitution of established specifications will not affect appearance, function, or durability, but will contribute greatly to economy. A drawer fixture, for example, costs approximately $80 or more per unit than one with sliding doors, and approximately $125 more than an open base unit. Considering that a 200,000 square foot department store may require hundreds of fixtures of this or similar type, the effect of the drawers alone on total costs can be seen readily to amount to between $50,000 and $75,000. The question to be answered in evaluating these fixtures, then, is whether drawers perform a function whose value will provide a proper return on an investment of that magnitude.

Another example of cost analysis concerns fixture protection.

Because hand trucks occasionally damage the corners of fixtures, some store chains automatically specify metal reinforcement on all freestanding fixture corners. However, the majority of similar, competitive stores throughout the country have failed to add this cost feature to their fixtures. Analyze the cost of adding these reinforcements versus the costs of repairing damaged fixtures over the years of operation. Such an evaluation might show that maintenance expense for a few fixtures is less than the cost of wholesale protection of them all. Extruded stainless steel corner reinforcement adds approximately $25,000 to the fixture cost for a typical branch department store, depending upon size and fixture density. Analyze this additional cost to be sure it's worth spending.

KEEPING FIXTURE COSTS DOWN

There are many ways of keeping fixture costs from climbing unnecessarily high, and the experienced store planner, architect, or designer is familiar with most of them. A fixture measuring five feet square as a single unit will save $90 to $100 as compared with two individual units of half the size placed back to back. A fixture with a removable base is $30 more than one with a built-in base. A metal framed showcase is approximately $300 more than one with wooden ends. The ends of fixtures that abut each other can be left unfinished; end panels can be readily applied at a later date if the ends are exposed. One note of caution: while cost considerations today require a constant search for less expensive methods of achieving the desired fixture function, take care not to compromise quality in the process.

"Quality" does not necessarily mean "embellishment." Some stores, such as high fashion specialty shops, do require fixtures which complement an overall ambience and relate to their couturier and other merchandise lines. But fixtures and ambience in a hardware store that should probably project a "no-nonsense" atmosphere, delicately detailed or couturier styled fixtures would be out of line.

Both types of stores, however, want fixtures of good quality and appearance to project their ambience. In fact, there is only one situation in which lesser quality fixtures is acceptable, provided the purchaser recognizes just what he's getting for his money. This applies to both one-time use and to temporary, seasonal use, where the need for the fixture will be brief and may not recur. Under such circumstances it makes little sense to invest in materials and workmanship designed to last twenty years; fixtures of this type should be considered expendable.

SELECTING THE RIGHT MATERIALS

Fixture selection includes evaluation of materials, workmanship, and weighing the advantages and disadvantages of different materials and finishes. Fixture manufacturers today use numerous metals and various types of wood, along with glass, synthetic boards, laminates, and plastics as component materials. Not only is the kind of material used important, but *how* it is used in the construction of the fixture, and for what component part, is equally important to the life span, maintenance, and ambience of the unit. After all, a fixture is an assembled product of parts joined together, and not all fixtures are assembled in a similar manner. However,

Figure 7-1   Store fixtures for displaying merchandise can be made from a number of materials: wood, plastic, metal, or glass. Here, metal tubular fixtures of varying heights provide an open, porous effect for merchandise that would be totally obscured if displayed on solid or opaque fixtures. (Dayton's, St. Cloud, Minn.)

many fixtures require hardware and decorative metal, legs, bases, drawer and door slides, finger grips, pulls, brackets, and standards. These appurtenances vary in appearance and cost, depending upon the material from which they are made. They may be stainless steel, bronze, aluminum, copper, or painted or baked-on enamel finishes on metal.

Figure 7-2 This mounted metal grid is a ceiling design feature that not only interrupts the broad expanse of ceiling, but also provides the supporting element from which improvised hanging fixtures are hung. The fixtures, which consist of two chains and a transparent plastic rod, are flexible, removable, easily stored, and offer total merchandise visibility. (Thalhimers, Raleigh, N.C.)

Metals

Among materials, metals vary in quality by application and intended function as well as in aesthetic contribution. (See Figures 7-1 and 7-2.) Stainless steel is both hard and durable. It can take abuse from customer traffic, hand carts, vacuum cleaners, and polishing machines. It is therefore widely used for the legs on fixtures, as well as in exposed areas and on corners. Aluminum is less expensive but also softer, affording less protection. Brass is quite soft and comparatively expensive, while bronze is somewhat harder; however, both have a tendency to tarnish and provide difficulty in assuring color conformity among the various assembled pieces of materials.

Brass and bronze are warm-textured, and so long as their disadvantages are taken into consideration, they can enhance the esthetic effect of fixtures when used as facing or trim materials. Steel is strong, easy to join, and readily machinable, but also subject to oxidation, so it requires a protective finish such as paint. Because painted metals provide a cost savings and allow an unlimited range of colors, they are being used for the metal components of fixtures. One drawback to this, however, is the tendency for the painted surfaces to chip on impact. Other finishes that possess a greater resistance to surface damage include mirror chrome, satin, baked or cold lacquer, and epoxy.

Woods

Multitudinous types of wood are used in the manufacture of store fixtures—some for their exotic and decorative characteristics and others for their functional qualities. All of these woods fall into one of two categories: soft wood and hard wood.

Soft and Hard Woods

Generally, soft woods such as pine are used for framing and under sheathing, but not normally for facings. However, some pines —ponderosa, for example—have been used as surfaces for lacquer or paint finishes. Pine is a stable wood product, resistant to bending, cracking, checking, and splitting. Sugar pine, in fact, can be made into panels as large as twelve feet long, permitting long face panel lengths with minimum joints. A major disadvantage of soft wood, however, is its vulnerability to abrasion and denting. It is also difficult to join into a rigid connection.

While all woods are subject to dents and abrasions, hardwood surfaces are naturally more resistant. Used as a facing, however, many (especially maple) tend to twist, bend, or warp even after being kiln dried and must be secured firmly to avoid these tendencies. As nosings and edgings, maple and poplar are excellent and, compared with other hardwoods, reasonable in cost. Both are easy to work and shape and take a good finish. Poplar comes in varied widths, lengths, and thicknesses and is readily obtainable up to 2½ inches thick; most woods are not available in this thickness. Poplar also tends to resist checking, splitting, and cracking, but is basically a utility wood not normally used decoratively. Maple is not only much more difficult to obtain, but also characteristically comes in narrower widths that require a great deal of piecing together.

The more costly and exotic woods such as rosewood do not necessarily insure durability. Teak is durable but also extremely difficult to machine and glue. Mahogany had its day in the early 1960's and has been used less and less in recent years, but it is attractive when finished and can be bleached to different color gradations. Also, mahogany panels can be obtained in good widths and lengths.

Plywood

In addition to being cut as solid members, woods are sliced in thin layers and applied to panels as a surface veneer material. Veneers are secured as facings to panels constructed in layers to form a core. Each layer, called a *ply*, is intended to strengthen the panel, and five-ply, seven-ply, and nine-ply panels are common. There is little discernible structural difference between seven-ply and nine-ply, and the seven-ply (approximately ¾-inch thick) is normally used for fixture panels. The tighter and sounder the core in plywood, the better; loose cores tend to show markings through the facings. Plywood panels permit the use of exotic woods as facings, which, as solids, would prove both prohibitive in cost and non-resistant to climatic changes. Application of paint or of plastic veneers to plywood panels must be done with extreme care to maintain equality of expansion and contraction, especially for such unsecured panels as sliding doors.

Synthetic Boards

In many instances, synthetic boards and panels have come into use as substitutes for plywood panels. One which has gained considerable acceptance is the flake or chip board, with a core made from wood chips and glue. The density and compactness of the core material establishes the quality of the board. It has many applications, but also some limitations. While screws can be secured in plywood panels, it is difficult to secure a firm anchorage in wood chips and glue because it is not a homogeneous material, unless they are of very high density. But used properly, the product resists shrinkage and warping and is economical. Unfortunately, some manufacturers use the board incorrectly in order to achieve competitive fixture prices, so buyers should specify the quality appropriate to the application.

Standard chip boards with plywood laminate facings are used for fixture backs, shelves, and sliding doors. Fiber faced boards, exposed and painted, are adaptable for valances and other applications. Shelving should have a core of proper density; this material is excellent for sliding doors or as a core for plastic laminated veneer panels. Where flake board joins flake board, however, a secondary member or frame should be used, because it is difficult to secure one panel to another. If the back of a counter is flake board, the sides should be plywood. Flake board is also adaptable as a counter or table top so long as it is largely secured by gravity and needs little anchoring. It should *not* be used when material strength is critical or when delicate machining and precise cutting and shaping are required.

One note of warning: The difference between economy flake board and better densities is a matter of a few cents per square foot. However, the difference in quality and construction ability is vast. If you are planning to use this material, consider the better quality. It is not a material with which it pays to pinch pennies.

Plastics

Laminated plastic is a fairly new synthetic veneer. It requires no finishing and minimum maintenance, comes in sheets of varied colors, and is highly durable as a long-wearing surface. A nearly perfect wood grain imitation is obtainable photographically, and plastic veneer wood finishes are commonly used to cut costs. Transparent or color plastics have also found their way into fixture fabrication. (See Figure 7-3.) They are used in clear, opaque, or translucent form and as laminates secured to a core or panel. They provide an enhancing material and give the designer a great deal of

Figure 7-3 The design concept of this shoe department uses transparent plastic fixtures instead of plywood, so that the customer's attention is drawn to the shoes on display rather than to the fixtures. The transparency of the fixtures gives the shoes a floating effect. (Thalhimers, Raleigh, N.C.)

latitude. The degree of tinting or color controls its see-through ability.

Clear plastic comes in several forms and types and, as a much lighter material, has been used as a substitute for glass. However, it is soft and vulnerable to scratching and discoloration. Styrene as a clear plastic has a tendency to turn yellow within a short time. Clear virgin acrylic will resist discoloration for many years if properly cleaned; ammonia and other chemical cleaners have a known yellowing effect. Reground clear plastic is developed from scraps of acrylic products. It has a yellow cast when it is manufactured and yellows further with age.

All plastics attract dust by static electricity, but there are antistatic chemicals which can be applied to the surface, which, if not washed off, will reduce dust attraction. Plastic laminates are best applied by hot or cold press. Surface-mounted or field-applied laminates installed without a press are apt to come loose.

Hardware

Hardware is an integral part of store fixtures. Although manufactured in various metals, cadmium or grey plate predominates. Companies give various names to the metal used, but all consist primarily of zinc plating, chrome plating, or cadmium plating. The important aspects of fixture hardware are appearance, price, durability, and matching with other metals. In the United States, hardware is fairly standardized throughout the country. Although there are varieties of standardized items to meet varied functional requirements, brackets and standards are interchangeable in most instances among fixtures of different manufacture. Standards support brackets, and brackets support shelves, rods, and miscellaneous components. Other hardware includes metal legs, drawer slides, finger grips, door slides, and drawer pulls.

Glass

Too often taken for granted by nontechnicians in specifications for store fixtures is the glass used for various components. Widely different types of glass are available, and each has a specific characteristic that makes it more adaptable to one specific use than another. Plate glass, for example, long known as quality glass with minimal distortion or imperfection, is slowly being replaced by a new material called float glass, which has comparable qualifications. Both are used for showcases, sliding doors, show windows, and other areas where clear, undistorted visibility is desired. Plate glass is still preferred for mirrors. However, they are both more costly than the sheet glass used for shelving and other less perfect items. Tempered glass is a safety glass which provides some personal protection when broken, since when it breaks, it shatters into relatively harmless fragments. Whenever glass must be used functionally where it is vulnerable to breakage, tempered glass will reduce the hazards.

FIXTURE SELECTION:
ECONOMY AND COST CONSIDERATIONS

A fixture, then, is an assembled product consisting of all these parts joined together by clips, fasteners, nails, screws, splines, glue joints, secondary frames, or panels. Each method requires its own degree of workmanship and therefore differs in cost as well as in its ability to withstand wear and tear. A fixture using splines, miters, rabbets, glue, screws, and glue blocks, including secondary panels and frames, is a quality fixture. By contrast, mass-manufactured units with minimal machine work using straight surface panels and held together by nailing and gluing results in fixtures of lower quality and with shorter life spans. The former carry a higher initial cost, but when replacement requirements are considered, provide

Figure 7-4 A combination of metal, wood, and plastic bin fixtures, each serving a different merchandise need, is used within the same shop. (Dayton's, St. Cloud, Minn.)

better long-term economy. Proper fixture selection, then, in addition to function, includes assessment of how the units are to be fabricated as well as what materials will be used. Modulated assemblage systems using interlocking members and hardware are prominent today for wood, plastic, glass, and metal fixtures. (See Figure 7-4.)

Fixture modulation, or systems using standard dimensions for both similar and varied fixture units, was mentioned briefly earlier in this chapter. There are several advantages even beyond the ability to transplant shelves, drawers, rods, and bins from one fixture to another. Standard dimensions reduce the number of assorted sizes and thus lessen both the number of spare parts required and the amount of space needed to store these parts, as well as the seasonal fixture components, when not in use. At the same time, the greater number of similar parts permits mass purchasing and consequent unit cost reductions.

Figure 7-5   A prefabricated "U" shape is the basic form used throughout this store. In cluster it becomes the wall fixture for hanging merchandise. As individual units it becomes the entry feature display. For greater ease of mobility and relocation, the module is kept below the ceiling. (Byck's, Louisville, Ky.)

Rapid changes in lifestyle and merchandise preference that began during the 1960's and continue today have played a major role in the development of modulated fixture systems. In order to react quickly to customer demands, merchants needed fixtures that are flexible enough to change with the merchandise requirements. Concurrently, the construction industry, attempting to combat the effects of inflation, began applying the module concept of standardized, interchangeable components to building systems. This achieved mass production economies and simplified installation. Both efficient and economical, it was only natural that this practice be extended to fixture fabrication.

Today, ceilings and floors are being designed to tie in with fixture modules. (See Figures 7-5 and 7-6.) The conforming ceiling modulation is usually based on the installation of ceiling track at a dimensional spacing equal to that of the fixture module. This ceiling

Figure 7-6 The modulated ceiling and fixtures provide for common assembly in both displaying and housing the merchandise. The uprights are secured to electrified ceiling tracks which provide the current for the spotlights. (Garfinckel's, Springfield, Va.)

track may or may not be electrically energized (there are degrees of sophistication available to the planner), but it is capable of supporting and anchoring a verticle pole or upright between floor and ceiling. Since the spacing between uprights conforms to the dimensions of the fixture module, fixtures or fixture appointments (shelves, rods, etc.) are easily secured between poles. If the track is electrically wired, it also can supply energy for lighting or other uses both to the fixture and to the general area.

This common design of interrelating ceiling, floor, and fixture originated in Europe and is known as the *Globus system.* Since it permits on-site change with little or no skilled labor, it has had growing acceptance in the United States by all types of retailers: chain and independent, discount and specialty stores.

Where a modular fixture system is to be used, the standard dimension selected must be considered carefully. It should conform with the fold of soft merchandise and with the common dimensions of hard goods to be displayed. Most important, it should relate to the standard available size of the material from which it is made. The latter eliminates the need for field or factory cutting and reduces waste.

Four feet has become the commonplace module today. Ceiling and floor tiles come in one-foot modules, and a multiple of four of these fits the four-foot module. Fluorescent lights come in four-foot lengths, while sheetrock and plywood panels are standardized at four-foot widths. A one-foot width generally accommodates most folded merchandise that people wear, while a two-foot width accommodates the soft goods fold of household linens, etc.

OBTAINING BIDS AND SELECTING A CONTRACTOR

With the type of fixtures and its specifications decided, the next steps are to get bids for the fixturing and to select a fixture contractor. Timing is most important here, since fixture manufacturers have definite peaks and valleys in their production cycles. These fluctuations affect both their prices and their ability to deliver their productions on time. The normal peaks coincide with construction schedules of stores which plan to open for three prime merchandising seasons: Christmas, Easter, and back-to-school. During these high production periods, the facilities, equipment, and manpower of most qualified fixture contractors are strained almost to the breaking point (and those of many less qualified ones beyond).

Like most businessmen, fixture suppliers are reluctant to refuse any legitimate order, so to meet peak schedules, they work overtime and must therefore charge higher prices. However, slack periods usually follow, and suppliers are then anxious to keep their wheels turning and to maintain their staffs of skilled employees. During such times, fixture costs may drop anywhere from 5% to 15% in competitive bidding. The cost of warehousing various fixtures for a given amount of time before installation can thus be far less than the additional cost of fixtures purchased at the wrong time. The slowest period for fixture manufacturers follows the Christmas season during January, February, and March. While they may be busy with field installation to meet and with the Easter season, the factories normally are quiet.

Usually a fixture contract awarded to a single supplier will prove more economical than subdividing the fixture work among several contractors. The magnitude of the total contract should provide the incentive for a lower price. But some contractors are better geared to manufacture particular types of fixtures than others, and occasionally a better overall price is obtained by assembling the prices from a number of contractors or subcontractors. There are dangers inherent in using a number of subcontracts, however, since a multiplicity of manufacturers means a further multiplicity of original material sources, so wood grains, colors, and metals used throughout the store may not match, destroying the store's ambience of oneness.

Manufacturers of store fixtures—or *fixture contractors* as they are known in the trade—are numerous, and the quality of their performance varies. No single qualification such as annual volume is enough of a reason on which to base the selection of a fixture contractor. As an indication of his capacity to produce, certainly volume is an important factor. But so is his available equipment and his ability to command sufficient skilled manpower, both in the shop and in the field, and to provide constant supervision and coordination with other trades. He must provide an end product that meets the specifications on which his bid was based, and any substitutions or changes should be carefully evaluated by the architect or designer to assure that they are truly equal to the original and do not result in an inferior product.

The contractor must also be financially stable. Contractors have been known to go into bankruptcy before completing contracts, not only leaving merchants without fixtures, but also causing the loss of a whole season's sales. And most important of all, a fixture contractor's past performance should indicate his ability to handle the size of the job and to provide the quality desired.

Ideally, fixtures should be installed immediately following the completion and drying of the store building. Since during their manufacture and assembly, fixtures are housed in heat and humidity conditions normal to our mode of living and working, they will be subjected to minimal changes in a completed building. Rarely, however, will a store await completion before starting fixture installation. Overlapping it with later construction phases gains opening time and added selling days. But unrealistically early installation can impose penalties.

Kiln dried wood, for example, both solid and plywood, has a moisture content of about 10%, and an accordingly strong thirst for any water vapor in the air. In properly air conditioned stores with relative humidity of 6% to 10%, the wood remains stabilized. But if conditions provide for an increase in the moisture content of the wood, permanent and expensive fixture damage can result. The moisture may come from any number of sources: from higher relative humidity in the surrounding air, unfinished wet terrazzo floors, plastering, leaks in unfinished roofing, unconnected or leaking plumbing and sprinkler systems, or improper drainage. When any of these possibilities occur, shelves will buckle; drawers and sliding doors will swell, twist, and bind; and fixtures may open at the seams or split.

Thus fixture installation schedules and overlapping of trades must be evaluated with extreme care to minimize the possibility of fixture damage due to premature exposure to store conditions. Since they hold and display the most important elements in the store—the merchandise—they are themselves the second most important element and should be treated accordingly.

Chapter 8

Store Ambience

"**Am'bi-ence** (ăm'bĭ-ĕns), *n*. That which encompasses on all sides." That's the dictionary definition of a word that has been bandied about quite freely, but is critical to the principles of store design. A definition derived from the glossary in the back of this book provides a better understanding of the term in store planning usage: "Ambience (Also called Atmosphere). The general quality of design which expresses the character of a store, resulting in an institutional personality immediately recognized by the consumer public."

Interior decor is the primary means by which the desired ambience is created inside the store. Everything that surrounds the customer once he has entered the store—the walls, the ceiling, the floor, the fixtures, the signing, the goods themselves—is an ambient element contributing to the customer's perception of the store's character.

AMBIENCE:
A MARRIAGE BETWEEN INTERIOR AND EXTERIOR DESIGN

A store actually consists of just two basic elements: the outside and the inside. And yet as a presentation to the buying public, these elements must present a sense of oneness. What the outside prom-

Figure 8-1 The design of this store combines a basic contemporary look with overtones of traditional styling such as a columned portico. This atmosphere of elegance and style, projected through this exterior, reflects the kind of merchandise sold inside the store. (Saks Fifth Avenue, Atlanta, Ga.)

ises, the inside must deliver. The exterior is the introduction to the store; from it, the customer should know that the store is a retail establishment, along with what type, and even what grade, of retail establishment. The interior must reinforce this impression, making a marriage of ambience, rather than two separate, contradicting elements.

All design elements, both inside and out, should also reflect the merchandise being sold. If it is a fine jewelry establishment or a high fashion dress boutique, there should be a delicacy of decor to match the goods being sold. Both the choice and the use of building materials should reflect the quality and type of merchandise.

An excellent example of this kind of interaction are the Saks Fifth Avenue stores. (See Figure 8-1.) Here there is a delicacy in the use of material: signing is subordinated; entrance motifs are subordinated; window displays are limited to give just a hint of the quality of merchandise contained within. The approach to the store gives the customer the impression of entering a salon. The character of the store building and its materials match exactly the character of the goods sold.

On the other hand, a large, multistory, full-line department store that carries both hard goods and soft lines would not reflect this delicacy; nor should it. This type of store's ambience should encompass an overall merchandising concept that projects to the public the fact that this is a large, institutional building, geared to carry tremendous assortments of merchandise. There may be more show windows, especially in a downtown location, and there will probably be wider entrances.

AMBIENCE AS A RESULT OF SHOP IMAGES

Although stores as a whole provide for a total ambience concept, we should remember that this total interior is a composite of many shops and boutiques, especially in large stores. The shops within a store vary by merchandise classification (men's, women's, children's, etc.) and by the style and quality of the merchandise.

Prestige stores as well as mass merchandising stores are subject to the same situation. One may find a range in the prestige store from moderately priced merchandise to the higher priced items in the designer's shops. The mass merchandising store may have departments that vary from budget to better merchandise. Whatever the range, it should reflect the image of the store. Image, after all, is the result of merchandise, planning concept, material use, color, and design motif used throughout; it is the store atmosphere that is created by the sum total of all the shop images in the store.

AMBIENCE WITHIN INDIVIDUAL SHOPS

Each individual shop, while adding to the overall atmosphere of the store, must also reflect the merchandise of that particular shop. For example, what would be the comparative ambience considerations in a men's shop versus a women's? Although color and styling have been heavily emphasized of late in men's fashions, men still prefer the darker shades and hues symbolic of their club atmosphere. The younger man, of course, seeks more vibrant color surroundings. The use of mirrored stainless steel, bronze, leather, natural woods with bright, strong color contrasts and strong design motifs: these are the usual basic ingredients for a masculine atmosphere. (See Figure 8-2.) Some outstanding men's shop interior designs have been attained through using these elements in tasteful and creative ways.

Figure 8-2 Modified traditional motifs using contemporary materials and design can be successfully combined to provide an elegant atmosphere for a men's shop boutique. The symmetrical modulated ceiling pattern, with its lighting fixtures and diffusers, within the confines of the surrounding walls forms a totally integrated concept. (Garfinckel's, Landover, Md.)

On the other hand, these ingredients would be inappropriate for a delicate women's boutique such as a lingerie salon, where a boudoir-like atmosphere would be more in keeping. Here the keynote would be a delicacy of materials, as well as color and refinement of motif. The silk and satin approach and the use of pastel shades would certainly be more appropriate than natural woods, leather, and bold colors.

Many years ago, Americans developed what they considered to be prestigious ambience, based largely on the authentic classic architecture they saw in Europe. At the time only the truly affluent traveled abroad. They visited the finer classic buildings and associated prestige with classic design. Thus palatial ambience was keynoted by such items as crystal chandeliers and sconces on the wall.

The native population in Europe, however, had been brought up with this traditional, classic design and architecture. Imitating these palaces and mansions rang false to Europeans, who saw authentic art and architecture all around them. They, therefore, trended more toward the contemporary look in retailing.

As travel became less costly and a wider segment of the public began to travel to Europe, more Americans began to join the retailers and their buyers who went to Europe annually on business or vacation tours. These people became very aware of the contemporary architectural trends in stores across the Atlantic, especially in the small boutiques.

At the same time, American youths became an overwhelming influence on purchasing patterns. The young demanded—and got—their own styling, both in merchandise and in the design of stores they patronized. No longer copying their elders, they, too, leaned toward the more contemporary, rather than traditional, look. Retailers recognized that the more modern approach was the ambience that would sell merchandise to the young, and store designs began to reflect this recognition, which still pervades the American retailing scene today.

THE RISE OF BOUTIQUES

It must be understood that in Europe, space is extremely costly. Boutiques occupy very small spaces because they simply can't afford higher rents. Many are in old buildings where the rooms are much smaller than we are accustomed to in this country. To get maximum utilization from these areas, therefore, these small boutiques became almost warehouses for merchandise rather than stores. Merchandise presentation was done in a very casual manner. The merchandise itself became the decor. Taking advantage of cubic content in these little shops, the merchants hung goods from the ceiling; they doubled up on hangrods, one above the other. If they had a niche, they put an accessory display into it. And while it was actually an enforced element resulting from the lack of available space in the small stores of Europe, the American buyers and traveling public thought this contemporary casualness was an innovative idea.

With the drastically increasing rents in today's shopping centers here in the United States, transferring this European trend to American shops has provided economic as well as design benefits. Greater merchandise density and a more casual merchandise presentation were adapted for large department stores as well as for smaller specialty shops. Oddly enough, in Europe, although the small shops were setting this trend, the larger stores retained their regimented, traditional character and did not adopt this casualness. American retailers, on the other hand, recognized its applicability to all types of retail outlets.

AMBIENCE SHOULD MEET CONSUMER TRENDS

The whole concept of design ambience, however, is transient; it changes almost from year to year. At one time, the predominent element was psychedelic color; then this was supplanted by super graphics, and then by a cubistic and sculptured trend. Whatever it is at any given moment, it must relate the tenor of the buying public's thinking. Stores went from patterns—on floors, on walls, even on ceilings—to simplified architecture based on sculptural designs and textures.

Thus design concepts have changed in the past few years with the introduction of features that will arrest attention on the floor as well as present and highlight the merchandise being displayed. In the past merchandise presentation was relegated for treatment against the wall only. Today, however, the peripheral and central areas of the sales floor are increasingly being married to provide a total store ambience that gives equal consideration to both on-floor and against-the-wall displays.

INTEGRATE ALL THE ELEMENTS OF AMBIENCE

All architectural elements, walls, floors, ceilings, lighting, materials, fixtures, and appointments must be integrated to provide a design concept that complements the merchandise. Although various shops within a store have their individual atmosphere, they belong to an overall total family concept.

Of course, no matter how they are planned, stores have certain characteristics. There's an overall ambience that encompasses the whole floor; and there are the individual shop ambiences and characteristics of the various classifications of merchandise. But there are other aspects to be borne in mind as well. The best store in the world is not comprised totally of 100% real estate locations within its periphery walls. Interior store locations, like commercial real estate locations, increase in value, depending upon the degree and frequency of pedestrian traffic. Within stores, customer traffic is a determinant in location ratings. The heavier the customer traffic, the greater the productivity of sales.

Where is the heaviest traffic usually found? On street floors, at the vertical circulation escalators and frequently used elevators, and at heavily trafficked store entrances. These are the 100% real estate locations. Under the best of planning, when every effort is made to minimize the situation, "cul de sacs," dead end areas, and remote areas away from the heavy customer traffic flow is still prevalent.

However, decor—ambience—as an abstract quality can raise the 60% or 70% location to 80% or 90% effectiveness. For example, the most remote point on a floor that is normally dead might be painted a bright contrasting color and highlighted by illumination. You'd be surprised how it comes alive. The decor can attract and bring people into space they might not otherwise shop. Thus ambience not only helps set the character of the store as a whole, but creates customer pull and helps to balance traffic patterns.

THE ELEMENTS OF AMBIENCE

Various elements and surfaces contribute to an overall ambience, and although discussed as individual entities, they should never be considered independent of the total concept. Rather, they should be thought of as harmonizing or contrasting with the other contributing elements. In fact, the evolution of a design concept should consider all contributing ingredients during the formulation of the design. Not only should the walls, ceilings, floors, and other integrated elements be considered in the flat layout plans, but they should also be studied from a three-dimensional approach. Perspectives will provide for a better interpretation of the relationship of all contributing items to the total ambience. Small scale models will further project the intended three-dimensional concept.

Always be careful of the dosage used. Judging colors or materials in small swatches and miniature samples can be misleading. A miniature square of gray material lying adjacent to a similar square of red material may be judged as an appealing combination. While this would compare colors, it would not show the degree or magnitude of color. Some colors by intensity carry more strength or weight, as often referred to in the trade. Colors should be balanced in weight. A small bright square of red may require an area several times its size in a light complimentary or contrasting color for balance. For example, a red tie with its limited surface can balance a gray man's suit of much greater comparative area. Reversing these colors, making the suit red and the tie grey would materially unbalance the weighted color relationship.

The same holds true in ambience considerations for the larger surfaces in stores. These include the walls, of course; they are at eye level and constitute one of the largest masses visible to the public. In perspective, another of the greatest areas seen by the customer entering the store is the ceiling. People do not tend to look up, but at certain angles in the distance, especially in a larger store, the ceiling is brought down almost to the horizon line.

The next big surface is the floor itself. A great deal of this surface is covered by fixtures, but still a large percentage of open area remains to be seen by shoppers. These are the three major surfaces that arrest the eye: the walls, the ceiling, and the floor. That's why the treatment of these elements are critically important to achievement of the desired ambience: they create the enveloping surroundings for the store's interior.

Although these surfaces are the most visual by area, the eye can be carried to any focal point desired by the proper use of color, material, form, and light. Large surfaces by size need not be the controlling factor in focusing attention. The treatment of large areas by the application of these devices—color, light, materials, and form—can serve to subordinate or emphasize these surfaces, as the ambience requires. However, due to the magnitude of surface, special care must be taken to utilize the devices properly.

One extremely important principle should be emphasized at

this point. That is, if there is a change in ambience, it must be confined. This applies equally to a change in styling or in color. If a change does not either blend with the ambience or utilize some logical technique of separation, it can injure or hurt the ambience of the store.

WALLS

Walls, because of their large surface mass and multifunctional use, have been one of the most abused surfaces in store interior design. As an integral part of an ambience concept, they have many stories to tell. Usually they provide a background for the shop or

Figure 8-3 These walls with their painted striping give this department an effective background for feature display of shoes and contribute to the boutique appearance of the area. Track lights on the ceiling provide both general and a feature spot lighting. (Garfinckel's, Springfield, Va.)

Figure 8-4 Colored plastic cubes, used as freestanding features, can be moved about to form varied groupings and configurations for on-floor display. The illuminated, colored recesses in the wall provide both an interesting design treatment and an effective merchandise presentation. (Saks Fifth Avenue, Houston, Tex.)

department, and a framing or home for the merchandise carried on or against them. (See Figures 8-3 to 8-5.) They should not be designed independently of all the other contributing elements, but should be made a part of the total shop concept.

In the open plan concept it is commonplace to use the walls in long, running strip fashion. Inasmuch as many merchandise classifications may border this strip wall, its related background changes with each adjacent merchandise group. Most often the color, material, and motifs change to indicate a new merchandise classification.

In viewing this unobstructed strip wall in perspective, we often find a patchwork of colors, designs, motifs, and materials. However, rarely does the customer view it frontally, where he or she would be limited to seeing the merchandise related to only one

Figure 8-5 Walls need not all be flat, plain surfaces above the merchandise that extend up to the ceiling. These curved wood slatted valances of varied heights above the merchandise not only contain the lighting that highlights the merchandise, but also add interest to the design concept. (Saks Fifth Avenue, Houston, Tex.)

classification, especially if there are no controlling visual or separating dividers to create barriers between ambiences. Instead, the customer may see a confusing array of displays. This is why physical interruptions are important: they avert visual conflicts in ambience. In fact, using physical barriers to separate ambiences is a principle that applies not only to strip walls, but also to shops and the walls that form their peripheries.

A Word of Warning

Before the store is completed, many retailers advise their designers, "This is the area set aside for family shoes." Pointing along a straight wall, they may designate one portion of the space for children's shoes, one for women's shoes, and one for men's, and they expect each to receive a different and appropriate decor.

The fallacy begins, however, when a mother brings in her son or daughter for shoes; she doesn't limit herself to the children's area, but sits in the first seat available. Such a mixture of decor is not only confusing, but also violates the principle of having one homogeneous design for the overall room or wall. A variety of designs here may be likened to a family living or recreation room in a home. No home owner would paint one corner yellow and place teddy bears and toy soldiers there just because the children play there, wallpaper another corner because the adults sit there for relaxation, and wood-panel still another to entertain guests at the bar. Such a mixture would create nothing but confusion. To avoid this confusion, the designer for the shoe department should have a homogeneous concept that avoids fragmentation and encompasses a total family shoe department.

The Function of Walls

There are many ways of treating walls. Remember that, if so desired, they can act as a reflector of light by providing a reflecting surface. A wall can be the element that holds the light fixture, the merchandise, or even the signing that identifies the merchandise classification. But it is also the element that holds the decor together. This decor can be applied decor, three-dimensional decor, paint, fabric, textural treatment, or paneling. It is the encompassing surface that confines a classification of merchandise and imparts to it a background. It is the most visible element from the greater portion of the sales floor.

A wall, then, "reads" both close and at a distance. Thus when visible from the store proper, it becomes an element of overall store ambience as well as an ambience contribution to the department itself. Any treatment of that wall, in its composite use, should be well thought out. This applies as much to lighting as to specific decor. The lighting may be affixed to the wall, it may be mounted off the wall but directed at the wall, or it may integrate the lighting with the merchandise fixtures. Decor may be applied to the wall; there may be signs hanging in front of the wall or on it; but all must be part of a single, unified design concept.

Interior Signing

Signing, or the identification of departments, is an element that relates to both walls and to other decorative aspects. Recognizing the constant need for change in retailing, the designer should not incorporate any signing if it may move seasonally, annually, or may be eliminated entirely. Many stores either do not use signs at all, or they use signs only with great discretion, depending upon the quality of store they are trying to project. However they are used, they should not be an afterthought; they must be carefully planned into the entire ambience concept as one homogeneous design concept.

Many stores in Europe, for example, eliminate all signing. Their idea of signing is a display of merchandise that will be visible to customers from the widest possible area of the store. This concept is being adapted more and more in this country. In line with this reasoning, a pillow department with an elevated display of fancy pillows would provide a classification identification with relative ease from a reasonable distance. Oversigned areas look like they are filled with billboards and are, ultimately, confusing. This is the last thing a retailer wants his store to project.

VALENCES (CORNICES)

For years, stores used valences along walls, and many still do. They provide housing for a source of illumination that projects light on both merchandise and on the upper wall area. (See Figure 8-6.) Psychologically, the lighting also adds to the general lighting of the overall sales floor, although there is little effect on actual foot-candle readings (depending, of course, on the color of the upper wall and its reflectability). However, there has been a tendency to overdo valences so that they look like an uninterrupted railroad track running around the store. If used in this fashion, they are monotonous, add little to decor, and permit very little ingenuity in adapting a method for lighting the periphery walls and merchandise.

When using valences, always keep in mind that lighting, since it is so important a tool in merchandising, must have a source that is integrated into the interior design. It must be a part of the functional

Figure 8-6   Indirect illumination behind the valances in this department both provides a wash of light across the garment and illuminates the wall behind and above the merchandise. (Gimbel's, Granite Run, Pa.)

ambience, rather than an element apart from it. Varying the height, width, or design of the valence may still maintain its function, but removes the monotony of a continuous run. Similarly, varying the approach to lighting merchandise and walls adds interest and flavor. Substituting or integrating a light track with flood or spot lights, for example, can offer an effective design and ambience change. Valences, then, while offering an effective method for lighting the merchandise below them, also run the danger of straightjacketing the overall design concept, lighting plan, and ambience as a whole.

The essence of good design is harmony or contrast. Verticals against horizontals, blacks against whites, lights against darks, reds against contrasting or harmonizing colors. If not properly designed, valences work against this all too often. They tend to cut the wall height into two parts, and thus restrict the design treatment. For this reason they should be utilized only under controlled design specifications, rather than in a flagrant, overall, monotonous usage.

FLOORING AND FLOOR COVERING

Floor treatments require extreme care in planning, since they vary in visibility, depending on the density of fixtures. One particular store I know of was designed with a beautiful blue carpet to harmonize with the decor. But there were so many fixtures on this carpet that when the customer stepped off the escalator, it was hardly noticeable, unless the customer looked directly down at his toes. So the contributing color was totally lost to the overall ambience of the floor.

Figure 8-7 Not all carpeting need be a solid color, texture, or design. In fact, patterned carpets can contribute a great deal to the ambience and design of an area. In this store, the weave of the carpet reflects the star motif of the metallic wallpaper and provides a young, exciting design for the department. (Saks Fifth Avenue, Boston, Mass.)

A flooring or floor covering is no contribution to decor when the aisles are narrow and the floor so densely covered with fixtures that at most angles the customer cannot see the floor, its covering, or its color. In any area where large surfaces of floor area are exposed and visible, whether it is carpeted, or made of wood, tile, or marble, then it becomes a much more effective contributing factor to the ambience. (See Figures 8-7 to 8-10.)

Figure 8-8   Marble flooring in both plain or contemporary patterns is adaptable for a variety of design concepts. This floor, with its inlaid diamond pattern, provides an elegant flooring surface that maintains the traditional design concept of the store. (Bonwit Teller, Eastchester, N.Y.)

With large floor areas, too, the planner must be careful when the floor is illuminated with down-lights, because many materials are reflective, and the color of the floor covering is reflected up on to the ceiling. Overlooking this aspect causes some stores to have different colored ceiling areas, entirely unplanned and often working at cross purposes with the desired ambience.

Figure 8-9 Parque wood flooring adds a note of natural richness to the home goods on display. The fixtures in the center of the floor provide interesting display presentations for the varied categories of items sold. The store is illuminated with high intensity lighting fixtures. (Steinbach, Pleasantville, N.J.)

Among the types of flooring, carpeted areas in particular are rich (soft of foot to walk and stand on for both customer and sales staff). They also have important functional aspects. If you take a white handkerchief and brush it against a carpeted area that's been walked on, for example, the handkerchief will remain basically clean. Do the same across a marble or tile floor, and the handkerchief will show dirt. The reason for this is that dirt and dust settle into the nap of the carpet, giving the appearance of a clean floor. Even with the same maintenance, other floors do not have this advantage.

Of course, each type of flooring material carries its own degree of prestige or quality, which should match the image which the store wishes to project. All are good products for their intended use. Certainly rich carpeting throughout would be neither appropriate nor functional in a store where shopping carts are used, such as a supermarket or discount store. If maintenance and wear and tear are the important considerations, then vinyl or wood might be chosen instead. Whichever floorings you choose, remember that while each type has its place, its contribution to ambience must also be kept in mind.

Figure 8-10   The herringbone vinyl simulated brick pattern flooring here provides an interesting approach to the adjacent shops that border this aisle. (Gimbels East, New York, N.Y.)

CEILINGS

Ceilings represent the third major surface of ambience. Especially in larger stores, the customer sees literally hundreds of square yards of ceiling area. A ceiling must meet many criteria. It must meet fire code rules. It must act to conceal air conditioning ducts and utility lines in most stores. It must provide the surface to which

Figure 8-11 General illumination may be either an inconspicuous element or a highly visible feature of a desired ambient effect. This highly decorative ceiling treatment maintains the ambience of this young people's shop and its avant-garde concept. (Garfinckel's, Springfield, Va.)

decorative features, signs, and lighting fixtures can be secured. And as a surface, the ceiling must be an integral part of the overall decor, treated in white or in color, with applications or hangings. (See Figures 8-11 to 8-14.) Since many ceilings support fixtures, both function and ambience must be considered with care in planning the ceiling.

First of all, ceilings should be designed to integrate the many elements they support—lighting, sprinklers, speakers, diffusers—in a set pattern. These elements shouldn't be located indiscriminately. The eye takes in vast areas of ceiling, and unless all these factors are treated in an organized approach, the impression as well as the functions of the items on the face of the ceiling can be chaotic. If the lights or the sprinklers weave all over, the effect will nullify the controlled ambience the designer is attempting to create.

There are many types of ceilings, of course. One is plaster, the standby for years. This is a wet application that is not often used these days. More common are the dry ceiling surfaces, sheetrock, acoustic tiles, metals, wood, and cork materials, depending upon the fire codes and the ambience. Within a room or a store, the surface of the ceiling by its very magnitude should be chosen for its contribution to the overall decor. In fact, its color alone is important, the texture or treatment aside. It's either a vast white field that compensates for other adjacent colors and acts as a unifying agent, or it's a vast color field or combination of multiple colors that contributes to each decorative scheme on the floor and walls from one area to another.

Many firms today are manufacturing tile ceilings that have

Figure 8-12 Ceilings properly designed can add significantly to the store's ambience. Here, a featured design is combined with functional lighting to create a skylight effect over the escalator well. The design on the ceiling is reflected along the rug border on the floor, thus relating floor and ceiling with a recall design. (Garfinckel's, Springfield, Va.)

patterned designs on the face or edges. Acoustic tile, in fact, might have a regress joint, exposed tees, or vee-joints on the corners. The planner must be careful in his selection that the ceiling design relates to the overall atmosphere desired and does not in any respect violate the design principles. And he must choose it with an eye to future maintenance and replacement of both the material itself and the accessibility of utilities above it and the elements that are attached to it.

Figure 8-13 The large expanse of ceiling area shown here is treated with squares of semi- and high-gloss reflective metallic paper to complement the contemporary concept. (Bonwit Teller, Chicago, Ill.)

Thus any component that contributes to the decor, whether it be ceiling, floor, or wall, must relate to a theme. It cannot be taken out of context by itself without impairing the design concept of the entire store. Lighting, of course, contributes mightily to the effectiveness of these elements and performs a decor function of its own. Let's consider this in more detail in the next chapter.

Figure 8-14 A mirrored ceiling can provide a reflection that creates interest and adds height to an area. What's more, here the reflective nosing on the sculptured ceiling defines the shop's area. (Stix, Baer, Fuller, Chesterfield Mall, St. Louis, Mo.)

Chapter 9

Interior Lighting

Without proper lighting, all other efforts at achieving ambience and design will go unnoticed. All merchandise selected and exhibited for sale; all efforts for a proper ambience; all attention paid in the formulation of interior design, color, display; and all textures and characteristics of materials chosen as part of a design concept are for nought if not properly illuminated.

Light, like a message, must be both sent and received. Different lighting sources and types of lighting fixtures transmit their varied light in different ways. The human eye "receives" light, and the brain interprets a "message." This message varies according to the design of the lighting system. It is for this reason that care must be exercised in designing the lighting of stores. Each design has a direct functional impact on ambience, decor, and sales. Each offers a message that can either enhance or detract from the store and its merchandise.

The intensity of illumination, for example, can either be so low that merchandise is difficult to see, or so high that the atmosphere of a particular area is ruined. While you want customers to admire the merchandise, a very brightly lit atmosphere can defeat the salon-like effect desired in a high fashion boutique, where elegance and homelike atmosphere is required. Again, tired shoppers who seek a quiet, subdued restaurant atmosphere away from the hustle and bustle of shopping may be disturbed by glaring lights. If you're selling television sets, high intensity lights can also overpower the picture tube presentation, thereby lowering both the performance and the sale of televisions.

Lighting of a store interior means more than just illumination. Interior lighting, particularly, performs three basic functions. The first, actual illumination of surfaces, is recognized and understood by just about everybody. The others are color rendition and the provision of contrasts through glare or variation of intensities. These are often overlooked by merchants and others involved in the construction of new stores whose expertise does not include the technicalities and the subtleties of lighting. There's little need, however, to dwell on the fact that people must be able to see where they're going and what they're doing, and to locate visually whatever merchandise they're apt to purchase.

Nevertheless, even the most simplistic discussion of the role of lighting in store planning and design does require at least a somewhat detailed discussion of the effect of various light sources on the perception of colors and textures; the use of different lighting techniques to perform specific merchandising functions; and the contribution of different light sources to the desired ambience of the store.

Inside the store, the source of general illumination, or the light level to which the eye will naturally adapt, is artificial rather than natural daylight. However, the principle is the same as it is out of doors. In an atmosphere of high illumination, spotlights and other individual lighting techniques will not stand out in contrast or be as obvious as they will when the general lighting level is relatively low. Since interior lighting is artificial and can be "custom made," however, the store planner can apply the physical and physiological properties of human vision to his own purposes: providing the proper ambience for his store and more effectively presenting the merchandise.

The perception of color by the eye depends on the source of the light reflected to the eye by the colored surface. Different light sources have different spectrums and emit light with colors of varying degrees of intensity. With some sources, the red end of the spectrum predominates; with others, blues and violets are emphasized. Some lamps come closer to approximating the color effect of sunlight conditions, while others come closer to the colder, more diffused effects of north light. Some even give a yellowish cast to the objects they illuminate, which is nowhere to be found in nature. These properties, too, are tools to be used by the store planner in designing a lighting system which effectively presents his merchandise and which contributes to the desired personality of his store.

THREE SOURCES OF STORE LIGHTING

Accepted standards of illumination have changed over the years. At one time as little as 12 foot-candles for store lighting was considered good illumination. Each year, however, light levels have climbed until today, where in certain stores, as much as 100 foot-candles or higher is an accepted standard. This is one reason, with the high cost of electricity, that other means of lighting, such as the fluorescent tube and H.I.D. lighting, have been developed.

Store lighting today utilizes three basic "families" of light sources: incandescent, fluorescent, and H.I.D., or high intensity discharge. Fluorescent and H.I.D. have come into popularity as the cost of energy has increased, since they provide illumination at reduced energy consumption. Incandescent sources include the common lamps (or bulbs) normally used in the home which are the direct descendents of Thomas A. Edison's original electric light, as well as tungsten-halogen lamps (otherwise known as quartz). Fluorescent lamps include a variety of developments, all of which operate similarly, but which offer varying color rendition qualities. The H.I.D. family members commonly in use in retail applications are mercury, metal halide, and high pressure sodium sources. Each has its own advantages and disadvantages, and proper selection depends not only on the properties of the individual light source, but also on its intended use.

In all lamps (also called bulbs) electrical energy is converted to light energy in order to provide illumination, but the mechanics differ. Incandescent light is produced by heating a filament through which an electric current passes. This takes place inside a glass bulb containing either a gas or a vacuum. The heat causes the filament to incandesce, or glow. Fluorescent and H.I.D. light is produced by passing an electric current through any of several different gases. The chemical composition of the gas determines the properties of the light emitted by the individual lamp.

Incandescent Light

Incandescent light has the longest history of use in stores, of course, and still retains many advantages over other, more recently developed types of lighting. First, many designers feel that incandescent is the artificial light which most closely approximates natural sunlight. Color rendition of fabrics and skin tones under incandescent light is warm and flattering.

In an incandescent lamp, electricity heats the filament, which is a very narrow wire inside the bulb. When the filament heats up, it radiates a concentrated point of light which casts shadows. This property enhances the three-dimensional form of the objects and merchandise it illuminates, bringing out the distinctive weave of a fine fabric, for example. Incandescent lighting also provides targets to highlight for points of merchandising focus throughout the store and will offer a pleasing effect of variety. A constant level of light throughout the sales floor can be as monotonous as constant ranks and files of identical store fixtures.

The concentrated point of light from an incandescent or H.I.D. lighting fixture, however, will create a darker ceiling ambience, unless it is supplemented with up lighting. This should not necessarily be considered a detriment; in fact, in better quality stores, it adds a note of elegance. For this reason most high quality stores today use incandescent lighting as their means of illumination.

Finally, since the same merchandise will look different under different types of light, incandescent sources provide the same light commonly used in the home, in restaurants and theatres, and in most places of social gathering. Consequently, clothing, furniture, and other goods purchased in an incandescent environment will retain the same appearance outside the store as they do inside. Their color spectrum will also appear almost the same as in sunlight.

Unfortunately, along with the benefits of incandescent lighting are several disadvantages. Since the filament in the lamp produces light by being heated to the point of incandescence, much of the electric energy consumed is converted to heat energy rather than light. Thus incandescent is the least efficient form of lighting in terms of energy consumed per given amount of lighting. In times of constantly rising utility bills, this is not a factor to be taken lightly. Not only does the heat produced by these lamps represent "wasted" electricity, but it can contribute significantly to the load on a store's air-conditioning system.

All lamps (bulbs)—not only incandescent—begin to darken in time. Incandescent lamps, however, do so even more quickly than tungsten-halogen. Thus they lose their initial intensity more quickly and have a markedly shorter lamp life than other types. This means that maintenance of desired lighting levels in an incandescent-lighted store will require more frequent lamp replacement, or *relamping*.

The tungsten-halogen bulbs are incandescents containing halogen gas. This chemical recycles tungsten back onto the filament instead of depositing it on the inside surface of the lamp and reducing its light output. Their value lies in almost constant light output throughout the life of the bulb, and except for emitting a slightly whiter light than regular incandescents and adapting to smaller light fixtures, they share the basic advantages and disadvantages of all incandescent sources.

Fluorescent Light

Unlike incandescent light, which is emitted from a concentrated point, fluorescent light is a more diffuse type of lighting. Because of its diffuseness, fluorescent lighting reduces shadows. The absence of shadows has its beneficial effects in locations such as stockrooms and offices, where shadows tend to interfere with the legibility of stockroom labels and other typical office routines. There are a number of different fluorescent lamps available which provide varying color renditions. However, because fluorescent light lacks the red part of the spectrum, it never reaches the flattering warmth of incandescent lamps.

Fluorescent bulbs are tubes that are coated on the inside with a substance called a phosphor and that contain a metallic gas, usually low pressure mercury vapor. An electric current passing through the gas causes an interreaction between the phosphor and the gas which causes light to be emitted from the tube. The chemical composition of the gas is a determining factor in the kind of light that is given off.

Since the tubes themselves emit light from their entire surface, installing the tube in a fixture that has a built-in reflector will increase the amount of light distributed downward. Along with the selection of light sources, lighting fixtures are thus an equally important element in the design of a store lighting system.

"But," you might ask, "if incandescent light is warmer than fluorescent, why use fluorescent lights at all?" The answer is that they have basic, practical, economic advantages. First of all, fluorescent lighting provides the greatest amount of light energy per unit of electricity of any light source currently available for store interiors. A far greater percentage of the electricity consumed is converted into light, with a corresponding decrease in the amount that is converted to unwanted heat. (Like the various H.I.D. lamps, fluorescent lights require a "ballast" through which the electric current must pass on its way to the bulb. This provides the amount of current and voltage needed to start and maintain operations in much the same way that a ship's ballast keeps the vessel on an even keel. Ballasts do consume a small amount of wattage which is transformed into heat, and this must be included in any determination of total electrical consumption by the lighting system. But it is negligible when compared to the heat generation of incandescent sources.)

At the same time, fluorescent bulbs have a much longer life span than do incandescents. Not only are they longer lasting, but they also deliver a higher percentage of their rated light output for longer periods. To the advantage of the lower electricity costs of fluorescent bulbs, then, are added the benefits of reduced maintenance, less frequent lamp replacement, and more evenly distributed light levels. These largely economic factors account for their widespread use in such relatively low margin retail establishments as supermarkets, discount outlets, and drug and variety stores. The pinch on store operating costs, along with improvements in fluorescent color rendition, have been major factors in their increased acceptance in department and specialty stores as well. Recently, with improvements in the color rendition of various fluorescents, however, they have been used increasingly as the source of general, overall lighting even in many fine department stores. Overall fluorescent lighting along with the judicious use of supplementary (or exclusive) incandescent light in various departments, both for spotlighting and for warmth, can provide the best of all possible worlds.

H.I.D. Lighting

The term "H.I.D." refers to all light sources in the high intensity discharge family; in retail applications, this generally means mercury, metal halide, or high pressure sodium lamps. Although less efficient than fluorescents in converting electricity into light energy, they are nevertheless more efficient than incandescents. While somewhat extreme claims have been made for the life of some H.I.D. bulbs, they are basically comparable to fluorescent lamps (and, of course, significantly better than incandescent).

Since technical developments of H.I.D. sources have concentrated on color improvements, many come closer to the warmth of incandescent lighting than fluorescent lamps can. Inside the store, H.I.D. fixtures look like incandescent fixtures. Since they have concentrated points of light, they also tend to produce shadows and emphasize the three-dimensional quality of merchandise much as incandescent light does.

Mercury lamps were first used for outdoor illumination where color correction had little or no significance. As their color quality improved, however, they began to be installed inside supermarkets and discount stores. Relatively inefficient (except by comparison with the incandescent), mercury offers a long lamp life of up to 24,000 hours, although light output diminishes quite rapidly. While color rendition tends to emphasize the blue part of the spectrum, the recent development of the warm deluxe mercury adds more warmth than any other lamp in the H.I.D. family.

Metal halide, on the other hand, is significantly more efficient than mercury and, except for the warm deluxe mercury, has generally acceptable color properties. Lamp life ranges from 7,500 hours to 15,000 hours, and the overall economics of a metal halide system come closer to fluorescent. This H.I.D. source, too, has both outdoor and indoor application.

At this stage in its development, high pressure sodium for retail stores can only be used outdoors, illuminating the parking area at perhaps the lowest owning and operating cost of any light source. While it is extremely efficient and has excellent lamp life (up to 20,000 hours), sodium has very poor color rendition. Since its tendency is to give illuminated objects a yellowish cast, it would clearly be inappropriate for store interiors, where the appearance of merchandise is so vital. In fact, where stores have used sodium in parking areas, people have actually failed to recognize their own automobiles because the color appeared so different.

LIGHTING FIXTURES

There are so many different lighting fixtures available for so many different light sources and purposes that it would be impossi-

Figure 9-1 Lighting can be incorporated into a design as a feature that provides both general illumination and a sculptural element of the shop. The abstract ceiling cubes here incorporate the lighting fixtures as well as relate the ceiling elements to the cubic design concept of the area. (Byck's, Louisville, Ky.)

Figure 9-2 Both wood flooring and chandaliers can add a note of elegance to either traditional or contemporary designs. Although traditional modified designs are declining, they are still being used in the better salons of prestige stores. (Saks Fifth Avenue, Boston, Mass.)

ble to list them, let alone discuss them, in a single chapter. In fact, fixtures are often specially designed to suit a specific application. There are, however, a number of considerations and techniques which enter into fixture selection and maintenance.

Primarily, a lighting fixture contains the electrical connection for the lamp (or *bulb*), holds and supports the lamp in place, and directs the light toward the area or objects to be illuminated. The fixture can be one of a long line attached to the bare ceiling supporting bare fluorescent tubes, or it can be recessed into a dropped ceiling with a lens cover that hides the lamps from direct view and diffuses the light source over the entire area to be serviced by the fixture. It can be a spot or floodlight mounted on a track to permit periodic changes in lighting emphasis, or it can be stationary. It can be a fancy chandelier or a simple socket for an incandescent lamp. (See Figures 9-1 to 9-3.)

The light emitted, unless a bare bulb or lamp is used, is depen-

Figure 9-3   The combination of H.I.D. lighting and track lighting provides general illumination for this shoe department and highlight the merchandise on display. (Steinbach, Pleasantville, N.J.)

dent upon the lamp and the fixture that houses the lamp. While a bulb emits 100% of its capability, it is the lighting fixture that directs this illumination to the surface or area desired. Not all lighting fixtures that function and look alike perform alike. They may vary from 30% efficiency to 70% or more. The reflective materials and items used in the incandescent and H.I.D. fixtures play a major role in the fixture efficiency. In fluorescent lighting, since it is a diffused source rather than a concentrated point of light, the fixture elements have less bearing on the efficiency of the fixture.

The long lines of exposed lamps in fluorescent fixtures covering a ceiling are called *strip lighting*. These are found most often in older supermarkets and so-called "bargain" stores, where the desired ambience projects lower priced merchandise and where the generally higher light levels inspire quick identification for purchasing decisions by customers. Even discount stores today, however, prefer to avoid the projection of "cheapness" and to provide an ambience that is more flattering to the merchandise. Thus, the trend has been established in almost all types of stores for upgrading appearance to recess fluorescent light fixtures into dropped ceilings in order to baffle the exposed lamp and reduce the glare.

Similarly, fixtures for H.I.D. lighting are being recessed into the ceiling. Since these lamps are more compact as a concentrated point of illumination, the fixtures are comparably smaller than those used for fluorescent lighting. Their distribution and light output (lumens, a measurement of light from the source) permits a wider spacing of fixtures, making them less obvious, while maintaining the desired light levels.

CEILING BRIGHTNESS AND HEIGHT

In store lighting the term *brightness* normally refers to the bright area of a lighting fixture that is visible to the eye when walking or standing about the floor. In order to reduce the brightness of lighting fixtures so that they will not blind a customer and thereby interfere with his merchandise selection, store planners do one of several things. They may recess the fixture into the ceiling; they may baffle the light source; or they may tint the collar around the fixture for light absorption. The smaller the fixture opening for a given light output, the stronger the brightness, if unshielded, and the darker the ceiling area appears in contrast. This is why some stores wash the ceiling in indirect light.

Overall ceiling brightness results from a mixture of the lighted and unlighted surfaces. This is similar to any fabric that is composed of two colors—say, black and white. The greater the quantity of black in the material, the darker the overall appearance of the fabric; and the more white, the lighter the material appears.

Ceiling brightness reacts the same way. The unlighted surfaces are like the black or darker components, and the illuminated surfaces are like the white or lighter areas.

One word of caution in planning your ceiling lighting: consider the customer's reaction to the store when he first enters. If he enters a street floor directly from the outdoors, the ceiling surface should not be too dark in contrast to the exterior brightness of sunlight. In situations like this, you might want to either provide up lighting to wash the ceiling, or to expand the brightness areas while controlling the glare.

Ceiling height is another contributing factor to the spacing of lighting fixtures. A light beam spreads according to its distance from its source, widening with distance. Therefore, lower ceilings require closer fixture spacing, while high ceilings, which permit wider light beams, can afford wider fixture spacing. The hung ceiling, with recessed lighting fixtures as well as the various utilities and mechanical systems out of sight in the space above, has now become most common in practically all types of stores.

Figure 9-4 The plenum is the space above the ceiling generally used for electric conduit runs, air-conditioning ducts, return air, sprinkler lines, and recessed lighting fixtures. The metal cross channels are the basic supports for the hung ceiling after all electricals and mechanicals are installed.

The space above a dropped ceiling is called the *plenum*. (See Figure 9-4.) It is an often-used gathering place for the return air being circulated by the heating and air-conditioning system and has a profound effect on the store lighting. On the plus side, the air movement tends to cool a significant amount of the heat which is generated to some degree by all light sources. This prevents the buildup of high temperatures, which reduce lamp life and cause ballasts to burn out. On the other hand, the air in circulation can deposit dust and dirt on both the lamps and on the reflective surfaces of fixtures, reducing their efficiency.

Cleaning, then, is critical for maintaining the maximum illumination for the expenditure. Regular, scheduled maintenance of both lamps and fixtures will keep dust and dirt from robbing a lighting system of its efficiency. At the same time, periodic replacement of *all* lamps in the store, timed to coincide with their effective lamp life (the point at which their light output has fallen to a predetermined percentage of the initial rating), is actually the most logical approach for maintaining the best efficiency. Certainly it is better than waiting for the lamps to burn out and then replacing them individually. Called "group relamping," this procedure results in a somewhat higher expenditure for light bulbs over a period of years, but realizes a much more significant savings in labor, relative to lamp replacement.

Wall Washing

The surrounding decor, especially the color of walls, may either absorb or reflect light. Lighter colors will make low light levels appear brighter, while dark decor will subdue and absorb even the brightest light.

Wall washing, as the name implies, is bathing the wall with light. This can be a very effective means of providing light ambience at relatively low cost. Wall washing creates the illusion of a brighter floor even though the actual on-floor foot-candle readings may remain the same.

In fact, the head of a prestige store complained recently about the poor lighting on his street floor. In measuring the light level it was found that the foot-candle readings were adequate, but that none of the walls were washed with light. This gave the illusion of a dark store. During the lunch period, temporary wall washes of the perimeter walls were introduced. Although the on-floor light reading did not materially change, it provided a psychological brightness to the entire floor. Upon returning from lunch, the store head could not believe that the lamp intensity had not been increased during his short absence. Even the customers asked, "When was the lighting changed?"

LIGHTING AS A MERCHANDISING TECHNIQUE

Store lighting, then, does not exist in a vacuum. It has a profound influence on all store elements. With the variety of light sources and fixtures available today, most large stores and even many smaller ones make use of their individual characteristics by mixing and matching different lighting for different purposes in different parts of the store. (See Figure 9-5.)

In Fitting Rooms

In ladies' fitting rooms it is vital to use the most flattering light source possible, regardless of economics, since this is the point of

Figure 9-5 The illuminated plastic pedestal in the center of the floor acts as a base for the feature display. The pedestal itself contains the lighting for the upper merchandise display. In the wall niches, display merchandise is featured through illumination from above. (Garfinckel's, Landover, Md.)

decision for most ladies' wear purchases. However, the light characteristics should not change too abruptly from one area to another, since the effect on the merchandise will be all too noticeable to the customer. The detrimental effect of such a change is particularly apparent in the meat cases of many supermarkets, which use light to reinforce the redness of fresh steak. Removing a package of meat from the case all too often results in an apparent quick change of color that can turn off even the hardiest of steak lovers.

Light to Create Moods and Add Interest

Light also helps create moods both directly, through its intensity and color, and indirectly, by illuminating the surfaces that feature a specific atmosphere; bright, high intensity lighting or illumination of vibrant reds or yellows tends to provide a more festive and gay mood.

Through contrast, lighting can bring out areas that may be remote or that may go unnoticed by store customers. At the end of an aisle or vista, for example, a brightly illuminated panel, color, display, or area that contrasts with the adjacent areas will tend to draw attention and traffic to what may be a dead or cul-de-sac area.

For years equal lighting distribution was a prime consideration for general store illumination. Today, however, many stores are reluctant to use equal lighting intensity as an overall blanket of light. Theatrical and dramatic use of lighting is now taking hold. Departments and boutiques bordering the major aisles are being highlighted, while the aisles themselves are being illuminated with less intensity and vitality. This tends to emphasize the shop and the areas where the merchandise is actually sold. Even within the boutiques themselves, the light level varies, highlighting displays and modulating intensities on the floor and wall to create greater drama and interest.

Lighting Garments

When illuminating merchandise and displays, care should be exercised to light the object correctly. The poor application of merchandise lighting can even detract from the merchandise. When lighting garments from a valence, curtain wall, or cornice that is approximately 7 feet from the floor, for example, make sure that the source of illumination is 9 or more inches from the outermost side or face of the garment. Too often the light source is hung directly over merchandise, so that while the light falls on the top of the garment, the front of the garment, which is the part most visible to the customer, is left in darkness. Light should wash the face of the merchandise exposed to the customers' view.

Figure 9-6 This salon is treated as if it were totally on stage. No attempt has been made to hide the lighting, which adds drama and excitement to the area. The lighting fixtures are totally flexible and can be focused on either the wall or the floor displays. The wooden floors add to this effect, providing warmth, naturalness, and theatricality. (Bonwit Teller, Chicago, Ill.)

Ceiling mounted merchandise lighting, either as track, stationary, spot, or flood light, should be approximately 3 feet from the face of garments for average mounting heights. (See Figure 9-6.) Remember that the spread of the light beam widens in proportion to the distance from the object. Therefore, with higher lighting fixture mounting, the distance from the fixture to the merchandise should be proportionately increased. While a beam of light should be positioned to illuminate the merchandise, it should not cast the customer's shadow on the merchandise itself. It should be placed to avoid having the customer view the item in darkness. It should also avoid angling the lighting fixture so that it blinds the customer who is walking toward its illuminated face.

Lighting Glassware

Glassware takes on greater luster when light is refracted through the merchandise. To achieve this it should be illuminated from directly above the merchandise, permitting the beam of light to refract through the object. (See Figure 9-7.) Glassware can have added sparkle with back lighting, base up light, or a combination of all of these methods. Glassware, especially transparent glass, takes on a crystal effect under such lighting conditions.

Figure 9-7 In glassware and stemware displays, illumination from the top and bottom gives the merchandise a crystalline, gem-like appearance. (Saks Fifth Avenue, Bergen County, N.J.)

Lighting Shelving Units

The use of one source of lighting for a multishelving unit is difficult. Should the shelving be of glass, some of the light will pass through from one shelf to another. However, a dense display of merchandise on any one glass shelf can obscure the light passage to a lower shelf, casting the lower merchandise into shadow. Glass shelving fixtures that carry a great deal of merchandise should not depend on passing light through shelves, but should use an angled light in front of the unit to illuminate the exposed face of the merchandise on each shelf. Since wood or opaque multishelved units cast heavy shadows from shelf to shelf if illuminated from a point above the unit, you should also use a projecting light in front for these, angled to fall on the exposed merchandise face of each shelf.

Although vertical light, modulated on the face of shelving units, has helped to light each opaque shelf, it is not always a satisfactory solution. Unless the merchandise is set back deep into the unit, the light will not illuminate the merchandise face. The merchandise must be pushed back, toward the back wall of the unit. If the vertical light source is in line with the face of the merchandise, the merchandise face will remain in darkness. Again, if the vertical light spacing is too far apart, the inside fixture area will be lighted only for a short distance on each side of the light source, and the center area of the shelving unit will remain in darkness.

The best solution for this is to illuminate each opaque shelf independently by placing a light under the shelf above. This has its drawbacks, however. It is costly, and unless a complicated electrical system is incorporated, lighting for every shelf limits the ability to readily adjust the shelf to whatever height may be required.

Show Window Lighting

Show window lighting depends upon its function. Lighting for show windows should be flexible so as to meet the varied demands of changing merchandise displays. The better stores use a valance shielded track light. Not only can this be used as an overhead track, but it can also be used vertically at times, hidden from view on each side of the window behind the proscenium frame. Here again, the light beam should be frontal, but not directly overhead, not only to insure the proper merchandise illumination, but also to avoid shadows cast from vertical down lighting on a featured mannikin, which distorts the facial expression and provides for a grotesque and distracting display. Stores also quite commonly install foot lighting in show windows, which is something like stage foot lighting. Sometimes back wall washes of light are used as well. This can be based on the personal desires of the display director.

Many of the more popular stores that have multimerchandise displays in their windows use fluorescent lighting of high intensity. Since this type of window does not feature limited merchandise, highlighting is not required. The lighting is therefore based on providing a high level of illumination over every square foot of show window that contains merchandise.

Chapter 10

Customer Services

Facilities for direct customer services generally take up space that could otherwise be devoted to merchandise. Therefore, they must be analyzed and planned with extreme care. The first of these is the provision for collecting the customer's money for his purchases. This is the basic, fundamental *sine qua non* of customer services in a retail store. No merchant in his right mind questions the need to provide space for this function, but how much space and how it's used should be calculated carefully. Customer services that are important in one store, however, can be eliminated entirely in another. This may include public toilets, lounges, and food service facilities.

Of course, coffee shops and restaurants are actually selling areas in which food is the merchandise. However, in the context of conventional retail stores, they are maintained as much to attract customers and keep them in the store to be exposed to other merchandise as to sell prepared food. At the same time, their demands on store planning are consistent with those of customer services generally.

CASHIERING AND WRAPPING

The most important customer service, cashiering and the wrapping of packages, varies with the type of operation. In stores where shoppers largely serve themselves, the facility often is a checkout, located either at the store entrance or at central wrapping desks located throughout the store. As the degree of customer service increases, the function varies from strategically sited cash/wrap stations, to individual department cash/wrap areas, to behind-the-scenes wrapping.

With a checkout, the customer brings his purchases to the checkout counter, where a cashier collects the money and either puts the goods into bags or otherwise packages them so that they are identifiable as paid for. This checkout system is almost always used in self-service operations.

Similar in function to the checkout systems are the central wraps, in which the customer brings the merchandise to a cashier within a department or allied group of departments. Central wraps are generally strategically located throughout stores in which the degree of self-service is somewhere between a conventional department store and a supermarket. As in the checkout system, the cashier's sole function is to collect the money and package the merchandise. However, with central wraps, both the quality and the type of packaging are often more versatile in that they allow for gift-wrapping or boxing as well as bagging. One advantage to central wraps is that it can cater to both types of customer service: self-service and sales staff assistance.

In most conventional department stores, a wrap and cash register is located on the sales floor, and the function of cashiering and wrapping is part of the sales person's duties. In some stores the sales person takes the merchandise to a behind-the-scenes cash/wrap facility and then returns with the packaged purchase and the customer's change or credit slip.

Another method is based on having the sales person escort the customer to the cash/wrap desk where the sold merchandise is handed to the cashier across the wrap desk, leaving the customer to wait and pay for the wrapped merchandise. This permits the sales person to return to the selling floor immediately, rather than waiting for the finished wrapped package.

The choice among these types of cashiering depends heavily on the type of store operation. Each suits a particular kind of store. And each imposes its own unique demands on floor space, equipment, electrical wiring, and store personnel. Some result in longer customer lines than others; usually the more classifications of merchandise that a cash register handles, the more customers line up at that point. If space is not provided for these customers, the lines overflow into the adjacent aisles and departments and disrupt the sale of merchandise displayed in those areas closest to the cash register. At the same time, displaying impulse merchandise wherever customer queues can be anticipated often means added sales.

On-floor cash/wrap tends to disperse the crowds somewhat, because each desk services a given area, rather than the entire store. This breaks the operation into a series of zones. The amount of space allocated depends on the required sales transactions, the number of departments, and the sales people it serves. High unit sales departments may have high volume sales but limited transactions. Fast turnover of merchandise, on the other hand, may require more cashiers and wrappers, and thus a larger cash/wrap facility or facilities. Again, the type of merchandise sold has bearing on the wrapping and cashier function. Accessories and fashion merchandise generate a need for wrapping and cashiering; major appliances and furniture sold from the warehouse, on the other hand, may not require any on-floor wrapping.

Locating your central wraps in strategic locations rather than in one central, concentrated location tends to reduce the number of customers at a given point. It also reduces the distance that sales people and customers have to walk. In addition, it gives the merchant flexibility, since some facilities can be shut down at certain times. While unused facilities might be considered a waste of space, they nevertheless permit an increase in cashiering capability by time of day, by day of the week, and even by season, thus facilitating the flow of customers to the cash/wrap services that vary with the sales transaction requirements.

One advantage in favor of the centrally located cash wrap, however, is the reduction of personnel. In order to be properly manned, three individual wrap stations may require three cashiers. However, with one central wrap, the job may be done by two wrappers assisting each other.

Central checkouts and even zoned, on-floor cash/wraps suit

self-service outlets such as supermarkets, drug and variety stores, discount stores, general merchandise stores with a high percentage of packaged and ready-to-wear goods. Conventional department stores, with a higher degree of customer service, tend more to individual sales-assisted cashiering, but even here an on-floor check-out is sometimes used in toy departments (especially at Christmas time) or record, book, and tape departments in order to exercise greater control. In large stores, a multiplicity of methods can be used from area to area and from season to season, depending on the merchandise. It is not necessary to have only one system throughout the store.

A word of caution about cashiering systems: once a routine has been established, it may prove difficult to change in the future. For example, one leading department store chain started with cashiers performing only this function, while sales personnel limited themselves to assisting customers in making selections. When a new branch opened, management experimented with using the sales people to wrap the goods and take the cash as well as perform their sales duties. The experiment was so successful that they tried to go back into the older stores with the combination sales/cashier system. However, they found it impossible to change; the attitude of the sales employees in the established stores was, "We were not hired to do cashiering; we were hired only to sell."

Many stores provide for flexibility by establishing temporary cash/wraps in space that is used for merchandise displays during slower seasons when the cashiering function is unnecessary. At peak seasons such as Christmas, utility outlets and fixture configuration allow them to easily install a cash register and institute the cash/wrap function where it is needed—but only when it is needed. This can be done most economically when the initial store planning and construction takes into account the temporary facility by building in the plug-in capability.

Like everything else in the store, cashiering facilities should be designed with customer convenience in mind. The easier the store planner makes it for the customer to buy goods, the more goods the customer will buy. Both cash and wrapping space and location should be integrated with the merchandise it services and the ease (or difficulty) with which the goods can be brought to the point of sale, either by the customer or by the sales clerk. Since a sales girl who accompanies the customer to the cash register (whether or not she handles the actual cash transaction personally) is missing from the sales floor during this time, the distance from the selling area to the cash/wrap will add to or detract from the amount of time she will be able to devote to selling merchandise, her primary function.

POINT OF SALE UNITS

Over the years architects and store planners have used the term *point of sale* to imply the last stopping point for merchandise that has been processed in the store. That is, merchandise on counters, in self selection fixtures, on tables, or hanging on racks has always been identified by store designers and planners as the point of sale. (See Figure 10-1.)

Figure 10-1 As gondolas and tables are disappearing in stores, more interesting multilevel fixtures are replacing them as the point-of-sale (POS) features. The varied heights and materials used provide appealing merchandise displays that help attract the customer's attention. (Stix, Baer, Fuller, Chesterfield Mall, St. Louis, Mo.)

However, National Cash Register recently adopted this term to relate to the consummation of a transaction at the cash register by calling this, too, a point of sale or POS. Thus, this term actually has two interpretations: one refers to the customer's selection of the merchandise for purchase, and the other, to the point of consummation of the sale of this merchandise.

A very important part of planning cashiering facilities for a new store today involves installation of the new electronic, computerized cash register systems, called point-of-sale units, and their effect on the rest of the store. As opposed to the old mechanical or electro-mechanical registers which recorded sales data on paper tapes, these point of sale (or POS) units communicate each transaction, either instantaneously as it is rung up directly to an in-store mini-computer, or by use of a magnetic tape cassette on which data is stored for later transmission to a central computer. Many also have immediate credit-checking capability as well, although some stores use separate terminals specifically designed to verify and authenticate credit card purchases.

When installation of an electronic POS system is anticipated, the store planner must bear in mind the additional equipment, besides the cash drawer, which must be accommodated. Often, this includes centrally located facilities physically removed from the register itself. The size of conduits and cables, not only to provide power for the system, but more importantly to transmit data to and from the POS terminal (as an electronic cash register tied in with a POS system is called) must be provided for in the plans for the building. If they are not, expensive changes will be incurred at the time of installation.

When the store itself is to be equipped with a computer, a portion of the nonselling area must be allotted for a room to control and oversee this function. This computer room requires special care in its specifications, since both temperature and humidity must be carefully controlled in order to assure the smooth functioning of the equipment. Sophisticated facilities of this nature are so sensitive to such changes that they will actually distort the information transferred and create havoc in the store operations if these considerations are overlooked. In fact, not only computers, but almost all electrical, electronic, and mechanical equipment will last longer and cost less to maintain if they are in an environment free of dust, dirt, temperature, and humidity. (See Chapter 11.) Thus, constant maintenance is absolutely vital to computerized systems. The degree of accuracy and control needed depends on the degree of sophistication of the equipment. Generally speaking, the more functions the system is capable of handling, the finer must be the control.

If the store is to be equipped with computerized cash registers, it is considerably more difficult to install these new cash register stations at a later date than it was with mechanical cash registers, since mechanical registers require only an electrical outlet, while the POS systems call for highly specialized wiring. Thus, a great deal of thought must be given to future needs. Even while this book is being written, my firm is planning for a 250,000-square-foot department store which will be so equipped. Such planning includes an analysis of year-round cash register needs. Possibilities of future expansion of the store as well as seasonal needs at different locations are affecting the store design from the very beginning.

PUBLIC REST ROOMS

If cash collection services are important to the merchant, another customer service facility can be equally urgent to the shopper. This is the provision (or omission) of public rest rooms or toilet facilities. An odd fact is that throughout most of the world, including the United States, codes or regulations requiring toilet facilities generally refer only to those made available to employees. Seldom is a commercial establishment required by law to provide such conveniences for the public (although labor laws insist on them for workers).

Different stores decide the issue of public rest rooms in different ways. For example, supermarkets or other establishments in which shopping is purposeful and not protracted seldom provide such facilities. Smaller stores in shopping centers usually rely on whatever community facilities there may be in the common area of the center itself or on those which exist in nearby major department stores. Few department stores in the past have been willing to rely on public lavatories outside their own premises. (This is not to be confused with the need for staff toilet facilities. Clearly, all stores need employee rest rooms, which keep departments and one-person operations from closing down during a time of need.)

Facilities open to the general public, that are neither a specific store facility under the store's control nor specifically for the convenience of customers, have disadvantages for the merchant, however. First, from a merchandising point of view, they draw customers out of the store, limiting their exposure to the goods on display and reducing sales volume potential. Second, the standards of cleanliness and security maintained in community toilets are beyond the store's control. Despite this fact, however, they can reflect adversely on the store's reputation if they are the only facilities available. On the other side of this coin, of course, are the maintenance and security efforts which must be exerted by the store on any rest rooms which it maintains on its own premises.

Most major department stores today, therefore, prefer at least some degree of in-store hygienic convenience for their customers. Even those which anchor modern, air-conditioned, enclosed malls where community rest rooms are reasonably well-kept and policed recognize that keeping customers within their own walls as long as possible is preferable to exposing them any sooner than necessary to the goods and services on view along the mall. However, fewer shopping centers are providing community toilet facilities. From an economic standpoint, shopping center developers prefer to rent the area and avoid the responsibility of maintaining and providing security for these facilities.

Generally, most merchants cater more to the needs of women shoppers than to those of men, since women generally spend more time shopping than men do. Many stores provide two separate ladies' room facilities, one for customers and one for employees, but only one men's room for both male employees and male shoppers. Others segregate employees' and customers' rest rooms for both sexes. (Separate staff and customer facilities eliminate the sometimes detrimental eavesdropping of customers on staff conversations regarding the store, its policies, and its operations.) Some stores separate the lounge area, where customers can relax, have a smoke, or primp, from the toilet facilities—occasionally even combining the men's and ladies' lounge. Such a provision is more usual for women than for men, however, due to the prevalence of women shoppers.

Construction costs and merchandising requirements combine to make such an apparently minor subject as rest rooms important for retail executives to study. Decisions on toilets and lounges should not be made lightly. For one thing, the decision may affect whether the customer stays in the store. For another, later changes may result in enormous construction costs. Among the building trades, plumbers command among the highest wages in most parts of the country. What's more, plumbing lines and fixtures are among the most expensive of all building components. Like everything else in the store, plumbing facilities which are discretionary (that is, not required by codes or labor laws) should be assessed in terms of the institutional customer services that the store wants to render, the indirect return they are apt to contribute in additional sales on the investment that must be made in them, and the space utilized.

At the same time, the store planner must locate plumbing in the building plan so that, while it is accessible to the customer, water supply and drain piping runs are reduced to the minimum. This can be done horizontally and vertically by superimposing plumbing functions above one another or placing them adjacent to each other. Peripheral sites off the sales floor adjoining employee facilities in the back room generally are the most efficient.

Toilet facilities are not flexible. To relocate them at a later date can prove costly. In planning toilet facilities, you should locate them against permanent walls or in areas that will not be subject to alteration or interfere with future interior store alterations by becoming an unmovable obstacle.

FITTING ROOMS

As with rest rooms, there is a variable between the requirements for both men's and women's fitting rooms. It has been a fact of retailing life that women tend to make their actual selection of merchandise in the fitting room, while men select and make their purchases out on the floor. The male shopper uses the fitting room to make a clothing change. Fit and acceptance of the selected garment are judged on the sales floor. The female, on the other hand, uses it in order to assure the fit of the garment and compare the way she looks in several garments. Thus the design requirements for men's and women's fitting rooms differ significantly.

Size, of course, depends on the type of store and the kind of merchandise being sold. A merchant selling bridal dresses, for instance, needs an oversized area to allow for the train, veil, and the likelihood that Mother's going to be there to look at the selection, so more than one or two seats are needed. Similarly, in prestigious salons the customer expects plenty of space and many mirrors, rather than a cramped little area. Some are decorated almost like living rooms, so that the customer can judge garments in the environment in which she is apt to wear them.

Mass merchandisers, on the other hand, seek fast transactions for quick turnover. Therefore, they must maximize the number of fitting rooms in a limited amount of space. However, fitting rooms are the points of the greatest degree of pilferage of wearing apparel. In taking this into account, facilities are limited to a minimum, and security considerations prompt an open design. Some simply have hung curtains; some have elevated the doors; some have look-throughs—all to give the store a measure of security without having the customer feel that she's standing in the middle of the sales floor.

Entrances to and from fitting rooms must be designed with care. When the rooms are placed in battery, you cannot control the customer who can enter at one end and exit from the other. Especially in stores with a large degree of self-service, there should be an attendant at a single point of entrance and exit at all times to assure that no more than three or four garments (whatever may be the store's limit) are taken in at one time and that the same number of garments is returned to the sales floor or taken for purchase.

As with merchandise display fixtures, the need for fitting rooms may vary according to season, such as during the bathing suit season. One method of providing them is to install temporary rooms or cabanas on the sales floor. Another method for either expanding or contracting fitting rooms in a given department is to expand into stock rooms adjacent to the sales floor for such purposes, provided they are designed to accommodate the temporary conversion.

Should a large battery of fitting rooms require two remote entrances for customer convenience, each controlled at opposite ends, the store should provide a fitting room aisle door midway between each end. During the slower business periods when only one entry is needed, the store can close and lock this door, so that customers will not enter from one point and leave through another.

Men's fitting rooms have different requirements from those of women. In men's fitting rooms it is important to have the proper clothing hooks and a seat or bench for the customer. The customer does not, however, need mirrors, because he views himself in the mirror out on the sales floor and is merely testing it for size in the fitting room. In most cases, a man has already made his decision about style when he enters the fitting room.

Security in the men's department, oddly enough, is more important to the customer than to the store, since men tend to leave wallets and cash in their pants pockets while they try on suits. Some stores provide little or no security for the customer in this regard; others provide individual keys for individual fitting room locks. The customer leaving his clothing and personal items in the fitting room can lock it and take the key with him when he leaves for the sales floor or for a fitting.

Generally, batteries of fitting rooms, especially permanent facilities, are best located on the periphery of the sales floor. Erecting them on the floor itself can divide a department and obstruct the view of merchandise on display. Temporary facilities such as cabanas, however, which are used only seasonally, may incorporate merchandise displays on the outside. Therefore, they can properly be placed away from the walls if they are designed and located so that they integrate with the overall store or shop layout and ambience.

Another factor to be considered, depending on climatic conditions of the location, is that fitting rooms should normally be cooler in the summer and warmer in the winter than most other areas of the store. In the summer customers trying on clothing tend to heat up and perspire more; in winter, since they will be removing generally warm clothing, they will be more susceptible to chills, especially if the fitting room is located against an outside periphery wall. Thus the best approach is to supply more cubic feet of conditioned air into fitting room areas to cool them in summer and warm them in winter. Alternatively, an electric heating coil placed in the supply duct with a thermostatic control will temper the air during the winter season.

Similarly, the lighting chosen for women's fitting rooms should provide the most flattering light possible to enhance skin tones and merchandise and to help create sales, since that is the point of decision for most women. The same characteristics of light should be used both on the sales floor and in the fitting room so that the color rendition does not change when the garment is taken from one area to another.

FOOD SERVICE FACILITIES

Food service facilities, whether lunch counters, coffee shops, tea rooms, soup or espresso bars, cafeterias, or full-fledged restaurants (see Figures 10-2 and 10-3) differ from other customer services in more than the fact that they are, strictly speaking, selling areas. While many stores, due to the nature of their merchandise, provide fitting rooms; all, due to health codes or to their isolated locations, provide rest rooms; and all must have cash registers, no store has to have a food service facility. This is entirely discretionary.

Usually, store hours are detrimental to a financially successful food service operation. The restaurant facilities within stores in the United States are seldom money makers. They require high investment in expensive equipment, they take up valuable area, and they usually realize only one mealtime's business per day. If there are

Figure 10-2   Some stores have sit-down restaurants with waitress service in bright, pleasant surroundings. (Diamond's, Tucson, Ariz.)

Figure 10-3   Many stores opt for the fast food type of restaurant with a snack bar and perhaps a limited number of tables. (Gimbels, Lancaster, Pa.)

late night openings, they *may* get a smattering of dinner customers. Thus the store is making the same investment as an outside competitive restaurant (which is taking advantage of two or more meals daily and longer hours of opening) without the benefit of the market potential. Some stores have tried to limit their menus and reduce the necessary facilities to produce those menus in an effort to minimize losses and generate a profit or a break-even return.

Despite the economics of a food service operation, many stores want such capability, even as a loss leader. They feel their food service is a potential drawing card from outside the store and a means of keeping customers within their walls that much longer. This is especially true in locations where there are insufficient good, competitive eating places in the vicinity. Most new stores today, however, are turning to smaller, simpler, and quicker food serving facilities. The limited menu of the coffee shop, tea room, or even stand-up fast food counters represent current trends. These provide faster turnover, take less space and capital investment, and still fill the desired need for this function of customer service.

Inclusion of any type of food service facility requires the store planner to understand the operation thoroughly, because food services vary. What is the service to be? What will be the menu? Will baking be done on premises? Will it be a sandwich and salad operation with minimal kitchen requirements, or a full-line, sit-down restaurant calling for a large food preparation area? The answers to these questions bear directly on the layout of the kitchen, the equipment needed, and the provision of such back-up items as grease traps, hoods, and vents over ranges, gas supply, and waste disposal.

Health code requirements will also specify what must be incorporated, but the planner must apply these as economically as possible, since food service is an extremely expensive facility and calls for costly investments in utility lines, mechanical equipment, and valuable floor space. All should be carefully planned in advance, because changes at a later date will prove even more costly in this area than in any other.

The number of store customer services is not limited to those mentioned in this chapter. Some stores have been known to include repair shops for jewelry, shoes, and handbags. Others provide travel and ticket agencies. Commonplace are lockers and package rooms. One may find post office facilities, bridal registers, optical and hearing aid facilities, beauty salons, barbershops for men and children, children's nursery areas, community rooms for customer use, check cashing and utility payment counters for telephone, electric, and gas bills, first aid rooms, etc. One well-known department store in England even provides for funeral services, apartment leasing and furnishing services, catering, taxidermy, and numerous other service functions. (See pp. 20 and 21 in Chapter 2.)

Chapter 11

Mechanical Systems

All too often, retail executives called upon to make decisions concerning the construction of new stores or the major remodeling of older ones tend to ignore the mechanical details. The technicalities of heating and air conditioning, of electrical and electronic devices, of escalators and elevators, and even of waste disposal equipment appear to have little to do with selling merchandise. "Leave this to the engineers," is the attitude of many merchants who simply assume that technical professionals know their jobs and will automatically fit the store's mechanical systems into the building's primary function as a selling machine.

Unfortunately, in the words of the Gershwin song, "It ain't necessarily so." The main purpose of the store may be to sell merchandise, but the idea is to do so *at a profit*. Aside from personnel, nothing affects the day in and day out operating costs of keeping a store open so much as its various mechanical systems. This is especially true in these days of constantly increasing utility bills, which have been forecast to keep on climbing indefinitely into the future.

At the same time, mechanical equipment and its installation

represent the greatest single portion of the total cost of a new store building. Thus the depreciation of this investment, whether it be part of the annual rental or direct capital expenditure by the retail organization, when added to the operating costs, becomes a major factor in the daily cost of doing business.

True, competent professional engineers and architects are well-versed in both the initial costs of installing mechanical systems and in their probable future operating costs. But what they may or may not realize fully are the sometimes direct but often indirect effects of these systems on the building's merchandising function. Mechanical equipment no less than display fixtures must assist the efficient operation of the selling machine in order to justify its existence in a store.

HVAC SYSTEMS

One of the most important of these systems is the heating and air conditioning. Since World War II, cooling in many areas has become as important to the operation of a public commercial facility in summer as heating is in winter. Whether it's a small shoe shop or a large full-line department store, a retail outlet without air conditioning on a hot, humid August day might as well close its doors; the customers will go where shopping is comfortable. Thus it is important not only to equip a store with year-round temperature and humidity control, but also to design and maintain the system in such a way that the possibility of breakdowns during extreme hot or cold weather conditions are reduced to an absolute minimum. (Chapter 14 outlines the different types of equipment and system designs and their maintenance considerations and effects on various types of retail operations.)

One of the most important points to remember about HVAC (as heating, ventilating, and air-conditioning systems are called) is that while all stores, regardless of type, should be so equipped, different kinds of stores are best served by different kinds of systems. Depending on the retail space to be temperature controlled, proper equipment can vary from a simple window air conditioner like those found in the home to various compact heating/cooling units (usually called *package* or *self-contained units*) on the roof, to a complex central plant which delivers heated or chilled water to fan units for warm or cooled air distribution through the ducts for an entire enclosed shopping center. Other systems deliver the humidity and temperature controlled air directly to the individual stores from a central plant.

For a freestanding store (that is, one which is not part of an integrated shopping center complex), the size and type of the retail operation are prime factors in the selection of equipment and the design of the system. (Of course, prevailing climatic conditions such as temperature and humidity at the site affect these decisions for *all* stores.) Generally, the smaller the store, the simpler and less expensive the equipment which can be applied satisfactorily. Similarly, the larger the store, the more equipment and the more complex the system design required.

CENTRAL VS. MULTIUNIT SYSTEMS

The multistory department stores with numerous boutiques and subdivisions have traditionally preferred central systems in which heating and cooling are distributed throughout the store from a single source. The central system usually operates on the principal of providing hot and chilled water to the various air distribution facilities on the floors. The alternate solution, which is used less frequently in multistoried buildings, consists of supplying conditioned air directly from a central distribution source. However, this is also more costly, due to the need for more duct work and floor penetration. Central systems often call for a greater initial investment in the plant and equipment, but they generally offer more economical operating controls which can more than compensate for the additional capital expenditure.

On the other hand, some major chains such as Sears and Roebuck have experimented with standardized building components for new two-level stores in an attempt to reduce the effect of extremely high construction industry inflation costs on expansion programs. Many of these experiments have included the use of several unitary heating/cooling units serving different zones of the store, rather than a single central system. The savings of such an approach are realized almost entirely in the initial cost, since the unitary equipment is factory-assembled, while most central systems (for stores over 100,000 square feet, at least) must be assembled on the job. Work done in a factory, of course, utilizes less expensive labor than that available on a construction site. Whether operating costs of such a multiple-unit system can be kept in line with those of a central system depends heavily on the store's ability to control closely their operation.

Single-level mass merchandising outlets such as large discount stores have long preferred the use of several roof-mounted heating/cooling units to central systems for several reasons. To these merchants, any detrimental effect which such equipment may have on the esthetics of the store's architecture is far less important than the savings they offer in initial cost. Low margins require low investments. In addition to less cost in equipment, it further economizes on long, costly duct runs.

At the same time, such stores usually feel they need offer the customer only *some* degree of comfort, not necessarily perfect comfort. Thus, if one unit should suffer a breakdown and be inoperative for a day or two while being repaired, the other units can shoulder a share of its load, keeping temperatures more comfortable inside the store than outdoors. This is an extremely important consideration when one realizes that a breakdown of a single source of heating or cooling without any standby equipment can force a store to shut down, while the existence of multiple units can better insure that it will be kept operative. Drug, variety, and general merchandise stores from 20,000 to about 80,000 square feet generally find the same advantages in this approach.

Smaller stores may take their heating and cooling from a single source, but their reduced requirements favor unitary equipment. This has the advantages of being the least expensive to purchase and the simplest to install, since it is mass-produced at the factory and needs only to be electrically connected and attached to generally simple ductwork in order to distribute conditioned air.

However, the very simplicity and wide manufacture of such units pose a danger to the unwary: since this equipment is so often selected on the basis of price, quality control tends to suffer. The merchant who saves an extra hundred dollars or more on the purchase price may find that he has to spend thousands more on repairs and replacements, that the life span of his smaller units is reduced materially, or, worse yet, that he is forced to close or to operate in discomfort because of a breakdown.

PROFESSIONAL ADVICE

Competent professional advice from architects, engineers, or experienced maintenance people is as necessary here as a guideline to proper investment in packaged heating/cooling units as it is in complex, applied equipment installations. Integrating the HVAC system into the merchandise function of a store calls for thorough knowledge of each portion of the store and how each area will be used. Besides supplying cooled and heated air, the system must be based on air circulation, requiring the removal of air from the conditioned spaces, depending upon their individual needs.

Fitting rooms require extra heating and cooling to assure that customers are comfortable while changing their clothes in winter and to keep perspiration to a minimum in summer so that clothes are not damaged. Candy and cosmetic departments need cooler temperatures to preserve the merchandise, while the heat generating lamp department, with its many illuminated lamps, also needs more cooling.

What's more, stores differ from homes in that customers dress for outdoor weather while shopping and are generally more active in stores than they are in their own homes. Thus, overall store temperatures should be maintained at lower settings than at home in winter, while they should be comfortably lower than outdoor temperatures in summer.

Oddly, during the winter season in a cold climate location, cooling may be required. During peak business periods when stores are crowded with bustling customers, especially those stores using high intensity incandescent illumination, the heat that builds up from bodies and lighting will generate this need. The best system is one that can be readily switched from heat to cool. The merchant should make sure that the engineer designing the system understands exactly the functional needs of the store and respects the desired ambience for every area of the store. Diffusers and return air grills should be integrated with the interior architect's design so as not to violate the design concept integrity, yet must not reduce customer comfort. In a quick, in-and-out purchase environment, there is less need for comfort than in a leisurely salon.

EFFECTIVE USE OF SPACE
ABOVE THE CEILING

In Chapter 9 we noted the prevalence of dropped ceilings and recessed lighting fixtures in retail establishments, and the utilization of the space above the ceilings as a plenum or gathering place for supply and return air, flowing either through ducts or through the plenum itself, which acts as an overall conveying duct. Of course, the supply and the return air cannot both use the plenum at the same time unless one source is through a duct, often insulated, to separate the two functions. Normally, the return is through the plenum and the supply is through ducts so that the proper temperature of air is delivered to the space to be conditioned. However, some systems today reverse this procedure; that is, they supply the air to the space to be heated or cooled through the plenum and return the air through ducts to the heating or cooling equipment. It is more difficult to control the supply of conditioned air when the plenum is utilized as a supply duct.

The use of space above the ceiling as a return air plenum has two basic advantages. First, the movement of the air around the lighting fixture removes excessive heat generated by the light source and increases the effective life of both lamps and ballasts. Second, it represents the simplest and most economical return air system, since it allows for the lighting heat to help supplement the heating system in the winter, thus reducing the cost of energy as well as the cost of expensive duct returns. (In the summer an exhaust bypass which dumps the excess heat outdoors can reduce the cooling load and lower air conditioning costs.)

HVAC SYSTEMS IN SHOPPING CENTERS

In shopping centers, many stores still must install and maintain their own HVAC systems. Some have a choice between installing their own equipment or tying into the central system of the shopping center by paying a charge to the center for either conditioned air or chilled or hot water and installing their own air handling fans and equipment. Both merchant and developer preferences vary on this point.

Let's take a look at two major national shopping center developers and operators as examples. One company prefers to serve all tenants from central systems, believing that economies of scale will benefit tenant and landlord alike. The other developer, however, generally requires each store in its malls to install its own separate system on the theory that the developer should be in the shopping center business, not in the utility business.

Among merchants, the preference is divided between those who wish to be able to control their own costs in the operation of individual systems and those who believe store personnel should be relieved of as many nonmerchandising functions as possible. Actual economy of operation can favor either approach, depending on the many variables at each individual location. When the merchant has a choice, these variables should be studied for an evaluated decision.

Many of the developers have benefited by providing the hot or chilled water or conditioned air to the tenant stores, thus deriving a profit from this operation. The tenant, on the other hand, does not necessarily pay more than he would encounter if he installed it locally within his own store. The magnitude of the central plant permits for a more efficient and less costly operation ratiowise per store than can be individually purchased by the tenant solely for himself. The tenant, in arranging that the developer provide these services on a charge basis and from a central plant, saves both in terms of the initial money outlay for equipment and in terms of whatever space in the store this equipment would have occupied.

Where stores must be equipped with separate installations for heating and cooling, the same considerations apply to shopping centers locations as to freestanding sites. The only difference is that in shopping centers one or more of the store's perimeter walls (and the mall entrance in enclosed air-conditioned shopping centers) usually abut adjoining conditioned spaces, so there is no heat gain or loss through those walls. This also applies to the ceilings of stores on the lower level of multilevel complexes that have stores situated above them. This arrangement reduces the heating and cooling requirements which would otherwise be necessary if the same store were freestanding and fully exposed.

Usually stores served by a central shopping center HVAC plant must still provide for the store's interior distribution of conditioned air just as though they had furnished and installed their own complete system, unless in the lease agreement with the developer, the distribution of air was an assumed responsibility of the developer under the terms of the lease. Usually heated or chilled water is delivered from the central source to fan-coil units in the individual stores, and the store's own ductwork then distributes conditioned air from these units as required by the merchandising layouts. As previously stated, fitting rooms located against exterior walls, with heat gain or loss to the outdoors, requires the installation of supplemental heating coils during the heating period and the delivery of additional cubic feet of air during the cooling season. Care should also be exercised in venting odor generating functions, where the return of foul air may be detrimentally circulated through the system throughout the store. Such areas as restaurants or snack bars, toilet facilities, beauty salons, and locker rooms should have the return air exhausted and not recirculated in the air conditioning system.

A common mistake made in the design of smaller mall shops, especially those with narrow frontages and deep interiors, is to use minimal supply and return air outlets not properly distributed. This often leads to pockets within the store, thereby creating insufficient air movement and customer discomfort. Professional engineering of the HVAC system is just as important for this kind of shop as it is for a major department store.

ELEVATORS AND ESCALATORS

Less of a mechanical mystery to most merchants than heating and air conditioning are elevators and escalators. Vertical customer traffic in multilevel stores has obvious merchandising importance. Elevators move far fewer people than do escalators, but an elevator costs far less on the market today. The escalator, or moving stair, can handle up to 10,000 people an hour, while an elevator has far less capacity. On the other hand, stores with four or more levels, especially in-city, high-rise department stores, find elevators more efficient and faster in moving customers to the upper floors. Today, most such stores are equipped with both escalators, for movement between adjacent floors, and elevators, for more rapid transit between widely separated floors. But elevators have become more of a customer convenience for those who prefer to use them, and for the disabled, ill, or senior citizens, or people with baby carriages, while escalators are more important to the mass of customer traffic.

Elevators today are as automatic as escalators. The trend away from operator control has become practically universal, and almost all elevators are push-button operated. Signing to identify the merchandise classifications on each floor is even being supplemented

Figure 11-1 An escalator should expose the customer to both wide areas of the sales floor and broad sections of merchandise. (Garfinckel's, Landover, Md.)

by tape recordings, which announce the features of each level and even promote special sales.

When escalators were first introduced, some of the more sophisticated, prestigious stores rebelled against escalators. They felt that moving stairways did not fit into the high quality ambience these stores maintained, and that the presence of elevator starters and operators added to the image of customer service. Today, however, the escalators themselves have become elements of sophisticated design and have not lowered the store's prestige image; in fact, they may be found in the highest quality fashion specialty stores. Regardless of whether you plan for escalators or elevators, however, they should be located so that they 1) do not obstruct traffic, 2) serve the customers efficiently, and 3) have a positive effect on sales. (See Figure 11-1.)

As far as the location of escalators, there are two lines of

Figure 11-2 This store chose to feature the escalator as a central element of transportation. The marble flooring with directional graining and veining provides a simple, rich flooring of natural texture and materials. (Garfinckel's, Landover, Md.)

thought today. One school of thought believes the escalator should not be featured, on the theory that customers, while searching for the escalator, will be exposed to a great deal of merchandise which they might otherwise have bypassed. The other school, however, holds that customers should always be aware of the location and presence of the elevator or escalator, just as they should be able to locate the store's entrances as easily as possible. The escalator or elevator is, after all, an entrance to other levels of the store. Customers can become irritated if forced to search, and irritated customers are not apt to respond to the exposure of merchandise when they are seeking the facilities.

Generally, however, escalators should be placed centrally, where they serve a maximum number of departments on all the floors. (See Figure 11-2.) In high-rise stores equipped with both elevators and escalators, and if the concept permits, you should be sure to locate both types of transportation adjacent or close to each other, thus giving the customer a choice of either within an integrated, planned traffic pattern.

SCISSOR VS PARALLEL ESCALATOR CONCEPTS

There is also a debate about whether escalators should be parallel or scissored. This is a question of whether customers should step off the escalator adjacent to the next escalator run, or whether they should walk around the length of the escalator well to pick up the next proceeding flight. Some stores hold that the customer's convenience is paramount, so a direct transition, without walk-around, is preferable. Others contend that this immediate approach to the succeeding flight causes the shopper to bypass merchandise on display.

Proponents of the scissor escalator configuration claim that this concept has greater flexibility and provides greater merchandise exposure and accessibility adjacent to each escalator landing. In ascending, the customer lands on one side of a floor and is exposed to adjacent merchandise. On descending he is exposed to merchandise on the opposite side of the floor. This scissor concept provides the option of switching the directional flow of traffic. Switching the flow permits the application of any one of the two systems: either the continuity of up or down runs or one that requires the customer

Figure 11-3   The scissor escalator concept

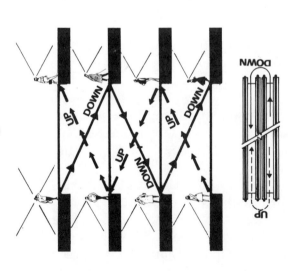

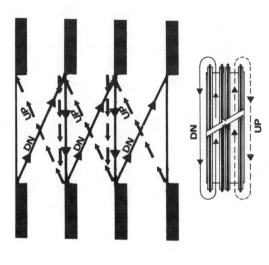

This concept permits a continuity of ascent or descent on adjacent escalator runs. One side of the selling floor is visible to customers going to the upper floors, while the other side of the floor is visible when they descend.

With this arrangement customers are required to walk the length of the escalator well to continue their ascent or descent. While this is less convenient to the customer than the adjacent runs, it provides greater exposure to merchandise.

Figure 11-4 The parallel escalator concept

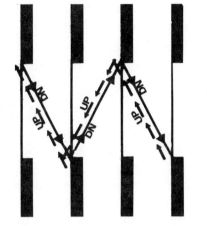

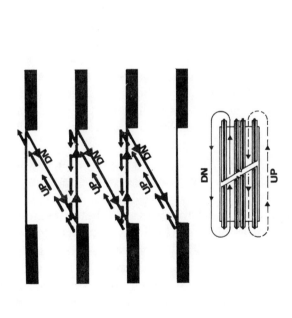

With this arrangement customers are required to walk the length of the escalator well, and are therefore subject to greater merchandise exposure on both sides of the floor and along the length of the escalator.

Using this arrangement, only one side of the floor is exposed to the customers on each landing, whether they are ascending or descending.

to circulate around the escalator to the opposite end of his arrival point on the floor, to continue his ascent or descent. (See Figure 11-3.)

Like the scissor concept, once the parallel concept is adopted, physical change is not feasible, except for switching the flow of direction. Parallel escalators (see Figure 11-4) can adopt one of two possible concepts. The first is based on providing alternating directions of adjacent parallel run escalators. In this concept the adjacent up and down runs are parallel on each level, but do not maintain a superimposed parallel relationship for all levels throughout the building. Thus whether a customer ascends or descends, he starts his continuing escalator run on the opposite side of the floor from where he started his previous run. The customer alternates from one side of the store to the other with each ascending or descending level. Giving the customer a continuity of ascent and descent, this concept provides the most direct route. However, it also leaves the side of the floor that is void of escalator approach unexposed to merchandise.

The alternative concept with parallel escalators is not only to parallel all up and down runs on each level, but also to parallel their superimposed positions throughout the building on all levels. With this concept, whether a customer ascends or descends, he begins his next escalator run at a similar point of location on each level. Although not the most direct route, this compels the customer to walk the length of the escalator well to the other side of the floor to ascend or descend to the next level. Thus customer traffic will be circulated around the escalator, similar to the scissor concept. Since this required walk will further circulate traffic from one side of the store to the other, customers will be subject to greater merchandise exposure.

In general, parallel escalators provide a better esthetic appearance than the scissor escalators, which have conflicting crossed runs and greater obstruction of visibility across the floor. However, the scissor concept is generally more advantageous, particularly for multilevel stores. By simple switching, either scissor concept is adaptable for changing flow direction. In two-story buildings, the disadvantages of parallel escalators diminish, since the runs terminate on the upper floor at handrail height and merchandise exposure is available at any point of arrival on this level. Additional escalator runs to upper levels do not block a view of the floor by another run. One thing a store planner and merchant should remember is that while the configuration—either scissored or parallel —cannot be changed, the flow of traffic can, since an escalator's direction can be reversed by simply pushing a button. (This is applicable to all concepts.)

Of course, even directional escalator change must be handled with care. For one thing, directional signs will have to be altered. More important, however, returning customers form identity patterns and habits in relationship to the store. If the familiarities keep changing, they become confused. Be careful, also, that in changing traffic flow patterns, you are not directing customers away from important merchandise exposure.

KEEP UP AND DOWN ESCALATORS CLOSE TO EACH OTHER

Merchandise classifications are placed on a floor based on merchandise appeal with the escalator approach in mind. Some stores tend to remotely separate the up and down escalators with the intent of subjecting customers to more merchandise accessibility as they move from one escalator run to another. However, rather than accomplishing this end, such placement tends to disrupt the continuity of ascent and descent and diminishes the unity of a single vertical circulation. In addition to this, separating escalators on a selling floor also consumes more space and generally increases the structural framing costs. For these reasons, it is best to keep up and down escalators close together or within a featured well opening. Many architect/designers are planning escalators in central courts or open well features that are neither parallel nor scissored, but rather placed at an obtuse angle to each other. This is primarily for design and esthetics.

ESCALATORS AND MERCHANDISE

Not all escalators are alike. They are constructed differently. They vary in appearance and specifications. Each must suit the desired function and ambience of the store. In addition to the variations in height and width, some are more noisy than others. Some have greater maintenance factors. Some have different ballustrades and handrails. Safety factors vary according to codes.

One important variable is width; escalators are manufactured in narrow and wide widths. The wide widths are usually four feet in dimension, but the measurement is actually from handrail to handrail, so the step lengths are actually about three feet, as opposed to the narrow escalator stair length, which is approximately two feet. The wider escalator has several advantages over the narrow one. For one thing, a mother and a child can stand beside each other on the same step, rather than one ahead or in front of the other, as is necessary on the narrower escalator. For another, it allows customers who are in a hurry to walk past those who are simply standing still on the moving stair. (Safety regulations usually forbid this, but a significant number of people pay no heed.) If a customer stands in position on a narrow escalator, he can block the forward movement of a whole line of impatient people, thus causing some customer irritation. The wider steps, then, are preferable. They also, of course, provide a more spacious and inviting approach to other levels. However, they're also more costly and take more space than the narrower escalator. Unless cost is a controlling factor, you should opt for the wider escalator, which permits additional increased customer traffic flow.

THE EUROPEAN ESCALATOR

European companies today are manufacturing a packaged escalator which is in common use abroad. Although extremely economical as compared with the American manufactured escalator, it has not gained popularity in the U.S. because of several reasons. Its angle is steeper, operating at 35 degrees versus the American 30 degree standard. What's more, it fails at times to fulfill all the code requirements at the location of the installation. It is therefore advisable to investigate the escalator and its specifications before purchase.

DISPOSAL OF WASTE

Both in shopping centers and in stores, one of the most neglected mechanical elements in both planning and design is the handling and disposing of waste. Yet, a successful store or shopping center has a tremendous waste problem.

Waste falls into several categories. One is wet waste, or garbage which is generated by supermarkets, restaurants, or other food operations. This requires its own unique methods of handling and disposal. Another is dry waste, which may be bottles and cans, cleaning debris, cartons, boxes, or waste paper. In one form or another, wastes are generated at almost every point along the retail pipeline for merchandise, from the receiving platform to the cashier's station. Facilities for collecting wastes, then, must be available to service each part of the store and throughout a shopping center.

For years, the most economical method of waste disposal for any sizable retail establishment was burning. Incinerators were the most common facility. Today's air quality standards and environmental protection laws, however, have largely resulted in a trend away from the burning of refuse. In some areas, more sophisticated, newly developed incinerators, which emit minimal pollution products into the air are permitted, but general practice is away from incineration. Thus, dry wastes today are removed from the premises either loose, baled, shredded, or compacted in giant containers.

There is a market in some localities for "pure" wet garbage, which is sold to pig farms, but this is rare in the United States. It also requires costly separation of wet and dry wastes, which may or may not be economically justified.

The movement to recycling has created markets for bottles, cans, paper, and especially corrugated wastes, but again, there is a handling cost in the separation of these materials, although in some areas the prices paid for them more than cover the cost of handling. Feasibility studies by several different chains of various types have established that marketing waste products can be quite profitable in large volumes, but also that each store and each region vary widely in this respect and must be examined thoroughly.

To the store planner, two factors are paramount. First, he must allow for the gathering and delivery of wastes from the different parts of the store to a central collection point. This can be done with hand trucks, chutes, or even sophisticated mechanical systems which convey wastes on belts or through pipes. Second, he must integrate his waste disposal system into the space available to him so that it does not consume any more valuable floor area than necessary. (His security director will be grateful if he also guards against the possible use of the waste disposal machinery as a method of egress for merchandise. It is far from unknown to find valuable goods carefully concealed inside bales of waste paper.)

In shopping centers, the problems are magnified by the number of stores. While the majors may handle their own waste disposal, the smaller stores require that the center itself arrange for internal accumulation and external disposal. If the interval of garbage pickup time is long, restaurants and other food operations should have a refrigerated wet garbage storage facility. Proper temperatures must be maintained so that the wastes do not deteriorate and generate odors. In addition, washing and hosing of garbage receptacles and cans should be a part of the built-in facilities.

Chapter 12

Back Room Functions

In order for the store as a selling machine to operate properly, it must be adequately supported by what are called the back room or behind-the-scene functions. To switch metaphors, there is no sense trying to pour more water through a funnel than can be accommodated by the neck of the funnel, and much of a store's back room, or nonselling area, acts as a funnel through which the merchandise, in order to be sold, must flow. No matter how successful a store's selling effort, a store cannot sell more merchandise than it can receive, or than it can take order for and ship. In designing new stores, many merchants, in their anxiety to maximize sales, make the common mistake of allotting too much space and attention to the selling floor at the expense of the back room space needed to support those sales.

OUTSIDE VARIABLES

Of course, the need for different back room functions varies widely, depending on the store's type of operation. If it is just one of a number of stores, some of the back room functions may be remote from the store building itself, reducing the need for nonselling area within the store proper. Conversely, the store may provide back room services for other nearby branch stores, thus increasing its ratio of nonselling to selling area.

A furniture department, for example, requires furniture repair facilities. If there is no warehouse or other place to perform this function, or if there is no larger flagship store to serve, space must be allotted for a back room workshop. If major clothing alterations are necessary, and there is neither a remote alteration facility within the company nor a place to contract the work out to, then space must be set aside for this function. On the other hand, if the major alterations are done centrally (as in a downtown flagship store), with only minor adjustments, such as hems or cuffs, altered on the premises, then back room requirements are reduced. Thus the back room variables are influenced by factors outside the store itself.

The merchandise sold also affects the design of back rooms. If there is a large china and glassware department, back room special wrapping is important to avoid breakage. Soft goods and hard goods impose different requirements. So do delivery policies; if certain classifications are shipped from a central warehouse to the customer after being selected from floor models at the store, both stockroom and shipping facilities can be reduced.

BASIC BACK ROOM FUNCTIONS

Back room functions can be divided into four basic categories. There are merchandise functions directly *related to the goods themselves;* there are administrative functions *related to management;* there are *employee functions;* and there are *operational functions* which affect the efficiency of the store both as a building and as a selling machine. Some of these can be fulfilled by facilities located remote from the store, while others cannot. In multistore organizations, many are served to greater or lesser degrees both in-store and off-site.

Conventional department stores offer the best example. Most majors today include a downtown flagship store from which the present company usually has grown, along with a number of branch stores, both in neighboring suburbs and even in distant cities. Prior to the advent of branches, the flagships were large, self-sufficient operations. The move to the suburbs and the growth of branch stores have materially reduced the sales volumes of most downtown flagships, however. As a consequence, these stores have found themselves with a great deal of space which could no longer be supported by sales. Many organizations faced with this situation have closed off former sales floors and converted this area into behind-the-scenes operations both for themselves and for neighboring branch stores.

Thus, as the flagship begins to function as a mother store for the branches, the back room requirements of the branch stores are reduced substantially. At the same time, the downtown flagship stores were generally constructed as high-rise buildings where building functions required a disproportionate share of the total space, and the selling area on the upper floors—the area most easily dispensed with—was converted to back room purposes.

Of course, it is possible to have the best of both possible worlds. The Broadway in Los Angeles, one of America's great department store organizations, has recently replaced its flagship with a brand new downtown store, designed and built more on the principles of a branch. It is not a high rise; it does not house the executive offices; nor does it function as a mother store for the branches. Indeed, along with the branches, the new flagship store receives back room services from a remote facility which is located on real estate far less expensive than that occupied by any of the stores, and its own back room is accordingly reduced.

NONSELLING FUNCTIONS

All stores—flagships and branches, department stores and drug stores—must operate with some back room area for supporting merchandise functions. Only the degree will vary according to the specific requirements of the individual store. Goods must flow from the supplier to the customer, and the store is physically the most important part of the pipeline. Merchandise is received, often marked, usually stored in a stock room, and then transported to the sales floor, where it is sold and either taken home by the customers, shipped, or delivered to them. Clearly, the store requires appropriate facilities to handle each of these steps.

Receiving and Marking

Receiving and marking represent wide variables, but this is the neck of the funnel through which merchandise flows. This is the input of goods; output (or sales volume) cannot be greater than volume received unless sold from catalogs or through telephone orders. Receiving facilities, to begin with, depend on the source of the goods received, the type of goods themselves, and the manner in which the goods are delivered to the store. The source of supply may be a chain's own central warehouse or distribution center, a consolidation center where small shipments from a number of different suppliers have been grouped together in a single large delivery, or directly from the manufacturer himself.

The sources of supply affect the required receiving facilities in several ways. A truckload of merchandise consisting of a variety of classifications such as might arrive from the chain warehouse or from a consolidation center must be sorted, carefully checked against the store's orders (sometimes several orders to several suppliers), and then either ticketed or not ticketed, depending on whether the individual items have been premarked at the source. A shipment directly from the manufacturer may be simpler, since it is apt to be a single merchandise category and represent a single order, but it is less likely to be already price marked (except for packaged goods sold at manufacturer's suggested list) and thus require in-store ticketing facilities.

Preparing Merchandise for Sale

Arriving garments may be already steamed and pressed and may arrive on racks, or they may be received in hampers or boxes and require steaming and pressing on the premises before being placed on the sales floor. Space devoted to receiving thus depends on the prepreparation of the merchandise, if any, and whether or not the goods can be moved from the platform directly to the sales floor or adjacent stock rooms with no further servicing.

In arranging for these facilities, the planner needs to provide flexibility, not only because of various sources and different merchandise conditions, but also because of the various seasonal demands. Receiving volume at any given time depends on the anticipated sales volume at that specific period. Thus the flow of merchandise varies according to the time of year in the back room, just as sales volume varies out front. Sometimes activity is extremely heavy, and at other times, extremely light. A receiving area, then, although specifically designated by function, should be able to expand and contract as needs dictate.

A point to be borne in mind in the design of receiving areas is that when the merchandise is delivered, delivery people are involved. The needs of these people also have to be considered. In large operations the drivers may arrive at the store after hours on the road, so toilet facilities should be incorporated on or near the loading facilities. In addition, the store should provide a proper station for checking the merchandise received to assure that the goods which arrive are actually the goods ordered and that they are all in good condition. Loading facilities should be located and equipped for the most efficient movement of the merchandise from the trucks through any processing areas such as ticketing rooms, and either into stock rooms or directly onto the sales floor.

Merchandise Distribution

Merchandise distribution is the inlet for merchandise. Once it's received, it's distributed through the store. The store must be designed to allow for transportation, either by racks, by hampers, or in bulk, brought up or down by elevator, carried by conveyer, or moved on rails. Some methods are simple, such as hand carts. Others are extremely sophisticated. Material handling systems also vary according to the size and function of the store and the types of merchandise handled. In a multilevel building, especially a major, full-line department store, both vertical and horizontal transportation of goods must be planned, and several methods may be employed.

For hangware, there has been a strong trend toward either manually or automatically operated monorails on which garments are whisked through the air from receiving stations to general storage, ticketing areas, and periphery stock rooms on the sales floor. Even small specialty stores are adopting this system of monorail conveyors for both transportation of merchandise and for an eye-catching display for goods in the front of the store. These can be as simple as the system used by dry cleaners—familiar to just about everyone—or fully automated and very complex.

In the last few years large stores have sought ways of mechanizing as many store operations as possible. The more sophisticated, electrically operated (and even computer-controlled) conveyors, monorails, elevators, chutes, or other mechanized equipment aids operate like a railroad classification yard, where a single man at a control panel (or, especially in large warehouses, a computer) can move varying classifications of merchandise on different tracks to different destinations simultaneously. If a shipment is destined for the ready-to-wear department, for example, it can be conveyed vertically and horizontally along the most efficient path to its destination without interfering with the movement of other goods. Such systems relieve congestion at the central receiving point by speeding merchandise out and into the various areas of the store where it is needed.

Another category of merchandise to be considered in regard to receiving and distribution relates to such items as major appliances and furniture that are sold from floor samples. Merchandise of this type is usually shipped to the purchaser, not from the store itself, but from a stock maintained in a central warehouse remote from the point of sale. Occasionally, shipments are made directly from the manufacturer. Only the samples must be physically received, prepared, and moved to the sales floor. Smaller but still bulky or heavy merchandise such as TV sets or stereos may also be sold from the sample, but picked up by the customer at a pick-up station adjacent to the stockroom somewhere on the periphery of the store or floor. Strictly speaking, then, not all merchandise sold in a store need flow physically through the store.

Shipping

Finally, back room requirements which might be needed in direct support of merchandise sales include a shipping and delivery area. Not all customers by any means wish to take all their purchases home with them. Garments may first require some alteration; an item may be temporarily out of stock except for a floor sample and require immediate delivery; the customer may lack the means for transporting the goods; or she may merely find it inconvenient to trundle her parcels around town on other errands. Other purchases may be destined for delivery as gifts and are not intended for the purchaser. When delivery service is offered to customers, then, planning concepts provide back room space and facilities for handling, packaging, and shipping merchandise, either by parcel post, by some such organization as United Parcel, or by the store's own delivery fleet.

ADMINISTRATIVE FUNCTIONS

Like merchandising functions, store administrative functions which call for nonselling facilities that vary widely. There may or may not be a credit department, depending on whether the store offers credit in one form or another. If it does, requirements to accommodate this can vary from a few square feet of the counter for a credit card imprinter (and no back room space) to a complete credit and accounting department where customers can apply for credit and pay bills and where all the processing of the store's credit operations is handled. The increasing use of computerized credit verification and data processing systems in stores which are involved in a large percentage of credit sales volume has led to a reduction in the space needed for this function within the individual stores themselves, and has guaranteed an increase in the credit operations performed in remote locations such as the mother store, or processed in executive office facilities completely removed from retail areas.

In a flagship or self-sufficient department store with no remote office space, requirements for executive offices, buyers, advertising, credit, accounting, and inventory control become massive, especially if they function for dependent branches. Of course, in a multistore organization, having these facilities in the parent store reduces the area required in the branch stores. This can realize tremendous savings if you consider how expensive real estate is in today's environment. The space devoted to administration in a branch, however, depends on the degree to which it can be served efficiently by a parent store or by a remote function some distance from the store to be serviced. For example, some merchants contend that buying for a particular store can only be done from that store; that only the buyer or the merchandising executive on the spot can properly interpret and anticipate buying influences within a given store's trading area. Others, especially large chains, prefer the purchasing power which a central buying office can exert, but allow individual store and district managers varying degrees of influence.

At the very least, however, all stores need a manager, and most higher volume stores have an assistant manager. Some area must be devoted to their space requirements, whether it be on a raised platform out on the sales floor of a supermarket or a suite of offices with a secretary in a fashionable department store. Other needs, where they exist at all, vary according to type of store. These include training facilities for new employees, personnel departments, and many other variable functions. Again, the degree to which a branch store will devote space depends on a function's distance from remote facilities, on company policy, and on size and volume of the store's operation.

OPERATIONAL FUNCTIONS

Nonselling space is also needed for operational functions, including security, maintenance, and housekeeping. Display departments in large stores must have sign-making machines and fireproof storage for paints. There must be places to keep light bulbs, ballasts, air-conditioning filters, and store supplies such as wrapping paper, bags, boxes, and sales books. Cleaning equipment and supplies also require area considerations.

EMPLOYEE FACILITIES

Employees in most regional locations of the country and in most types of stores need locker rooms, lounges, toilet facilities, often a lunch room, and even some recreation area. The store personnel, after all, are a competitive item in retail operations; it is through them that the store's personality is directly or indirectly transmitted to the customers. Many stores cater to employees in order to raise morale and to keep good employees by setting up congenial facilities.

The space and requirements devoted to any or all of these functions must be decided on the basis of each store's individual characteristics, including size. No rule of thumb is applicable in all situations. Some relationships are, however, typical. These are best illustrated by the sample branch department store statistics which appear on pp. 74–75 in Chapter 6. While not universally applicable, the list of back room or nonselling functions and the space allotted in that particular branch may be considered typical of many stores of that size.

Chapter 3

Retail Security Programs

Security is the function of protecting the store, its contents, and the people in it from various hazards. Loss of merchandise through theft, either internal or external, is the specific hazard on which most retail security programs focus, but losses due to fire, floods, storms, or earthquakes (affecting both the merchandise and the store building itself) and protection of employees and customers on the store premises are also proper concerns of a comprehensive security system.

The greater portion of a security program is operational in nature and functions through personnel, rather than through equipment or through the physical composition of the store. This is of concern to the store planner only insofar as his design does not impede security operations. Indeed, full coverage of security requires whole books,* not single chapters. Here, discussion will be limited to security considerations in the design and construction of new stores.

---

* Among the best being the two volumes, *Security Control: External Theft* and *Security Control: Internal Theft* by Bob Curtis, Lebhar-Friedman Books, 425 Park Ave., New York, N.Y. 10022.

THE SERIOUSNESS OF CRIMINAL SHRINKAGE

Perhaps the most important point to be understood about security and its vital effect on the success of a store is the enormity of the shrinkage problem throughout the retail industry. Shrinkage, of course, is an improper word. It refers to the difference between the retail value of goods actually received and the cash value actually collected for them. It can occur in a variety of ways: spoilage or damage done to merchandise which renders it unsalable; honest (and dishonest) mistakes made in either price marking merchandise or in reading price tags incorrectly, resulting in the merchandise's being sold for less than its retail value; the switching of price tags; and—by far the largest category—the actual theft of the merchandise itself. Estimates (there are no accurately documented statistics) place the retail industry's losses due to criminal shrinkage (internal theft, shoplifting, burglary, price-switching) at more than $1 billion annually.

Many retail operations feel their security program is performing good if shrinkage amounts to less than 3% of sales, and some actually boast of containing it to 1% or less. Many books and articles have been written about security. If these percentages seem hardly worth mentioning, you should remember that a department store chain doing a $100 million volume would experience a $1 million loss even at 1%. And those are bottom-line dollars which are deducted from profits. Obviously, security measures which effectively guard against shrinkage are worth both careful consideration and some significant investment.

PERSONAL SERVICE

Probably the security program most effective against shoplifting would incorporate a sales staff large enough to greet each and every customer entering the store with a smile and a cheery, "Good morning. May I help you?" Those six words are among the most powerful deterrents possible to a thief; more powerful even, than all the electronic gadgets in the world, since they put him or her on notice immediately that somebody is paying attention. At the same time, they offer the honest customer the ultimate in one-to-one service, and there can be no resentment. Unfortunately, it is not economically sound to staff a store with anywhere near that large a personnel-to-customer ratio, and other devices, some of which must be provided by the store planner, are required. Whatever the staffing, however, sales clerks should be as visible and as security-conscious as possible.

DOORS

The logical first step for the store planner toward building security is to consider the building shell. How many openings does it have? Doors have been placed to maximize customer access to the selling area, as well as to assure the efficient flow of merchandise into the store. But wherever customers or goods can enter, merchandise can leave, both legally and illegally, so a large measure of security control must be exercised near and around doors. The more doors, the less overall control. Any access with borderline value, where a customer *might* want to enter the store or which *might* be useful in receiving goods should be eliminated.

While wearing his security cap, the store planner should think of these points as leaks rather than as entrances to the store. (Of course, an extremist security man with a one-track mind, given his head in store design, might construct an hermetically sealed building which nobody could enter or leave from, so the merchandise inside would be safe forever. But that hardly serves the basic function of a store as a machine for selling goods.)

Within the store, doors and access points to various areas should be given equal consideration. The same principle applies to a fitting room, a jewelry department, or a stock room as to the store building itself: the more doors, the less security control is possible. Fitting rooms have been discussed in Chapter 10, but along with toilets, they are the shoplifter's favorite place for secreting merchandise on his or her person. Thus, the fewer points of entrance and exit for fitting rooms and toilets, the easier to keep them under surveillance.

SECURITY REQUIREMENTS VARY FROM DEPARTMENT TO DEPARTMENT

Different departments located on the sales floors have different security requirements. Higher priced merchandise, especially in small sized units such as jewelry, cameras, and many electronic items, is usually displayed in cases to which only store personnel have access and placed in highly visible locations. Even in mass merchandise stores with central checkouts, such departments have their own cashiering facilities, so that no goods leave the display area until paid for, at least in theory. Other departments, especially in stores with a large number of intimate boutiques, arrange displays and fixtures to fence off their area, so that the point of access and egress is narrowed and security control is enhanced. Even in the more open zone and cluster concept, displays and fixtures can provide a measure of traffic control by serving security without hampering primary selling functions.

BACK ROOM SECURITY

In the back room, security is attained for especially sensitive merchandise (jewelry, small appliances, electronic goods, furs in general merchandise stores, cigarettes, liquor, cosmetics in drug stores and supermarkets) by segregating the areas where these goods are stocked and limiting access to them to specific personnel. Here, behind the scenes, security is concerned not with shoplifting, but with employee pilferage, or internal theft. Some experts place shrinkage losses due to internal theft throughout the retail industry as high as, or higher than, those due to shoplifting.

AN EMPLOYEE PACKAGE ROOM

Many stores maintain a package room for employees. Here, an employee coming into the store with a package or suitcase, or an employee making a purchase during the day deposits his package with a security man who holds it until the employee leaves the store. This room is most logically located as close as possible to the employee entrance, near the time clock—a station which should be continuously manned during business hours in a major store. This method provides honest employees with the convenience of a check room to safeguard their property, while it deters dishonest employees from augmenting their property at the store's expense. Usually no packages at all are allowed in the locker rooms, since this would make the store and the use of locker rooms even more vulnerable to pilferage.

THE RECEIVING AREA

The station for checking shipments in the receiving area should be located so that there is constant surveillance of the loading docks as well as of all other entrances and exits of the store and the back room. There should never be an open or unlocked door which is not continuously visible to someone charged with the responsibilities of making sure no goods leave without authorization.

SECURITY ON THE SALES FLOOR

Out on the sales floor, security is best served by wide visibility; the more visible a shopper is, the less likely he is to become a shoplifter. (See Figure 13-1.) In some ways the store planner must resolve

Figure 13-1 This feature display permits visibility into the salon, but restricts the totally open front. By limiting the access and egress, the store can add to its security without the appearance of barriers or controls. (Garfinckel's, Landover, Md.)

a basic conflict between security considerations and merchandising functions. There is an increasing economic need in moderately priced merchandise stores to increase merchandise capacity into fewer and fewer square feet of floor space. This is being accomplished through the increasing use of more cubic space by going upward with shelves and merchandise displays. But the higher the fixtures, the more it obstructs overall visibility.

From a security point of view, constant fixture heights of about 4½ feet, which is below eye level, would provide ideal visibility throughout the store. But constant heights are monotonous, and ambience as well as the store's merchandise capacity are affected. Designers are resolving this conflict today by recognizing that the eye can only see so far before confusion sets in. This generally applies to very large, mass merchandise stores with the open plan concept.

DESIGN CONCEPTS THAT CONSIDER SECURITY

Design concepts for new stores should incorporate all elements required for proper merchandise presentation including fixtures, displays, and decor elements to focus attention on a specific merchandise classification. This should be accomplished without violating security. Merchandise presentation includes placing goods against walls, hanging them from the ceiling, supporting them on and around columns, and displaying them as on-floor fixtures. If these elements are carefully located, besides enhancing the department and displaying merchandise, they should assure that there are no pockets or hiding places where dishonest customers will go unobserved. In so doing, not only is security improved, but other classifications of merchandise are made visible to the customers. Thus proper planning serves the best interest of both merchandising and security.

SECURITY IN BOUTIQUES

In fashionable boutiques where design calls for intimacy rather than visibility, sales staffing performs the security function. A store planned on the shop concept tends to restrict a sales clerk within her own department, rather than encouraging her to intersell from one department or another, so her constant presence is a deterent to shoplifting.

HOW DESIGN CONCEPTS AFFECT SECURITY

Finally, the store planner can attain both visibility and the benefits of increased cubic capacity without obstructing total visibility by incorporating porous and transparent fixtures as dividers between shops, whether these be open filligree work, clear plastic fixtures or decor elements, or any other features which give the illusion of separation without completely closing off the area to sight. (See Figure 13-2.) This permits a higher stocking and display of some classifications of merchandise without sacrificing security

Figure 13-2 Transparency eliminates any obstructions to visibility, thereby improving security. These fixtures, constructed of glass and plastic, permit total visibility of the merchandise from all viewing angles of the shop. (Saks Fifth Avenue, Houston, Tex.)

needs unnecessarily. The customer can see the merchandise, and the staff can see the customer.

When the store is planned according to the zone and cluster concept, actual walls can enclose an entire zone, since this will include enough allied departments to assure constant staffing, and sales clerks who can intersell from department to department, providing security within the zone. This gives the designer an opportunity to create an ambience for that zone which can have individuality, thereby separating from the adjacent department, while it maintains security within it.

SECURITY DEVICES WITHIN THE STORE

Security staffs in many store chains work closely with store planners, not only to consult on the effects of fixture heights, department locations, and other aspects of store design, but also to include certain built-in methods of surveillance. These include two-way mirrors, cat walks, false columns, and other hidden vantage points from which store personnel can observe customers without being seen themselves.

The idea, however, is not to disclose their whereabouts, but to make the public conscious that these devices exist. Customers should be informed by every means consistent with the personality of the store that hidden watching posts exist, so that even when sales personnel are not visible, a shoplifter cannot be sure he isn't under surveillance. The same principle applies to the use of closed-circuit television (CCTV) cameras and other sophisticated security devices. The investment in such equipment is justified, not by the apprehension of shoplifters, but by their deterrent effect. Prevention is the primary aim.

There are many new developments in electronic security control for retailers, from CCTV to sensitized tags which, if not removed from merchandise at the time of purchase, trigger alarms when they leave the store or a designated zone. A discussion of their application and of their pro's and con's belongs more properly in a book on security, rather than here, since—other than their actual installation and use—they have little effect on the design and construction of the store.

Similarly, stores are beginning to employ programs to educate the public about the detrimental effect of shoplifting on retail services and prices; to train employees through security programs and controls; and to participate in the activities of a security department. Such programs are operational in nature and independent of store planning and design. The store planner's security responsibility is to design, locate, and construct the elements of the store, to incorporate them, to maximize security control, and to provide as wide a range of visibility as possible consistent with the store's desired ambience.

Chapter 14

Store Maintenance

Maintenance, like the poor, is always with us. A store must be attractive and must have all its elements functioning, not only on opening day, but on every day it expects to do business. The costs and facilities required to keep up all its component parts can be greatly reduced and more completely controlled if maintenance is carefully considered at the time the store is first designed and constructed. This means paying close attention to the likely costs of operating and maintaining each element throughout the life of the store, as well as to the initial cost (or installed purchase price) of the materials, equipment, and workmanship specified at the time the store is built.

STORE COMPONENTS REQUIRE MAINTENANCE

A store, after all, consists of hundreds of different components: the exterior, the doors, the glass, the floors, the ceilings, the walls, the fixtures, the lighting, and various mechanical systems. Everything requires some degree of maintenance. The air is filled with dust and dirt that settles on surfaces. The movement of both people and merchandise deposits further foreign matter, as well as creates wear and tear. Mechanical equipment has moving parts which can deteriorate through friction and through abrasions from external sources. We don't live in a vacuum.

The more often something is used, the more it is exposed, the greater its vulnerability to wear and tear and to dust and dirt. Naturally. Some materials are more resistant to abrasion and corrosion than others. Thus a general philosophy in the selection of materials for surfaces should include maintenance considerations as well as considerations about the esthetics and function. Too often, ignoring maintenance makes the least expensive item the most costly in the long run. This is true for both moving parts and static surfaces.

THE STORE'S EXTERIOR

Starting with the exterior of the store building, the most vulnerable areas are where people can reach, with respect to both normal dirt and graffiti. Materials in such areas should be easily cleaned and maintained. Higher up, weather and local air quality affect the store exterior. Rain and snow carry dust and dirt; changes in temperature cause expansion and contraction; and air pollution deposits oily acid and salty films, which not only mar its appearance but actually cause erosion of the building materials and veneers.

ENTRANCES

Metal and Wood

Entrances require several kinds of maintenance. People's hands, in gripping, pulling, or pushing on the metal bars or panels in manually-operated doors, for example, present a special problem. Human hands secrete an acid which turns bronze, brass, and other metals to tarnished relics of what the designer had in mind. This, of course, applies to other elements of construction that is handled frequently throughout the store, such as drawer pulls and showcase railings, stairway bannisters, and handrails. If made of metal or wood, these surfaces should be guarded by protective coatings like lacquer, both to reduce discoloring and tarnishing and to make maintenance easier and less costly. Of course, some metals can be tarnished by the impurities in the air, and where these must be used (to suit the desired ambience or for other reasons), they should be coated for protection regardless of whether they come into contact with human skin.

Glass

Again at the entrance, the glass in the doors and adjacent show windows is vulnerable not only to dust, dirt, condensation, and smearing through contact with people, but also to breakage. In recent years laws have been passed in many communities requiring glass in such areas to be tempered to resist breakage, and treated so that injuries are reduced when it does break. Based on the principle of automobile safety glass, such glass crumbles into particles with fewer cutting edges than ordinary glass.

Flooring

In stores that are subject to frequent customer traffic, especially in climates subject to rain, snow, and sleet, the floor of the vestibule or entry is going to take an awful beating from wet shoes, rubbers, and boots. The flooring specified should therefore be able to withstand this kind of abuse. But the specifier must also be careful that such areas, when wet, do not have too slippery a surface. Highly polished marble, for example, might be resistant to wear, but it can also contribute to falls and injuries.

Within the store's selling area particular consideration should be given to floors with the heaviest traffic. These include the areas adjacent to entrances, around the escalators and elevators, stock room accesses, and of course the aisles, which bear the burden of both customer traffic and of hand carts and racks transporting merchandise to the various departments. Materials for these areas should be resistant to the abuse of heavy traffic. When wear does occur, the flooring should be able to be easily replaced either entirely or in limited sections.

Selection of such materials should take into account not only the people burdens on them, but also the ease with which they can be cleaned and—a point often overlooked—to their resistance to the wear and tear imposed by the cleaning operations themselves. They must be able to withstand the soaps, detergents, or other chemicals used in washing and waxing and the abrasive effect of various machines used to apply them. They shouldn't turn yellow or become brittle or crack due to housekeeping care. Too many floors have lost their initial color, changing from white to yellow or even brown because of the effect of detergents upon their surfaces.

When selecting a floor tile, the store planner should make sure a design or texture is not limited to the surface of the tile, but is carried through its entire thickness. A textured floor has been known to lose its design and surface color within a few months of wear when limited to surface treatment only. While the texture in all of the store's shops remains pristine, the aisles can quickly become dull, colorless, and patternless due to the wear and tear of customer traffic, cleaning operations, and scratches and pock marks from umbrellas and women's heels. This is especially noticeable in elevators, where there is a heavy concentration of people.

Of course, selection depends on ambience. It would be as improper to design a store according to maintenance considerations alone, with no thought to ambience, as it would be to ignore maintenance entirely. But decor and maintenance need not be in conflict. A carpet, for example, often supports luxurious ambience and has practical advantages as well, but selecting the correct commercial grade is important.

In addition to providing an upgraded ambience, carpeted floors have practical applications. One additional benefit is their softness under foot. Because of their cushioning effect on the feet, carpets are less tiring for both the customer and the staff than the hard surface floor covering. Since no merchant wants either to impede or limit shopping because a customer's feet are tired or to hamper sales staff enthusiasm because they are foot weary, carpeted floors can offer multiple benefits.

WALLS

Like floors, the maintenance of wall surfaces must also be carefully considered. Walls adjacent to an aisle will be brushed by people or bumped by hand trucks or other equipment, making them vulnerable to wear and tear. The surface material must therefore be capable of withstanding this kind of activity. Washable vinyls, plastic veneers, and other recently developed products can more readily resist these abuses than other materials.

In selecting these more resistant materials, however, do not overlook their contribution to the overall design and ambience of the store. Some materials can be more readily cleaned than others and are more resistant to abrasion. While the initial investment may be more costly, the longer life span of the product can make it more economical in the long run. All surfaces that are subjected to heavy traffic adjacent to them and are within reach of people require special maintenance considerations. These areas include the surfaces of columns, the areas leading to escalators, the lobbies of elevators, fitting rooms, and halls where delivery of merchandise takes place. Kitchen and toilet room walls should also be constructed with washable surfaces to maintain sanitary standards.

CEILINGS

The ceiling is a vast surface, and although horizontal, it is a dust collector. Air moves across the ceiling surface from a number of sources. Usually, heating and air-conditioning diffusers are on the ceiling, and the air returning from the sales floor is drawn through the ceiling to the plenum to the heating/cooling source; since the filters are positioned to clean the air before it is heated or cooled again, return air usually contains impurities. Warm air rises as it is displaced by cooler air, thus carrying dust and dirt with it to ceiling surfaces. Furthermore, people servicing mechanical systems above and on the surface of the ceiling who change a light bulb or ballast or who hang or replace signs subject the ceiling to some abuse.

Generally, porous surfaces are required for acoustical purposes. Fissures and porous facings trap and contain the sound waves, thus absorbing sound; the reflective sound from a flat, smooth ceiling surface, on the other hand, can project a similar impression to being on the inside of a drum. However, every little porous hole or fissure is also a dust and dirt collector, so care should be taken to specify materials from a maintenance standpoint, as well as for its functional acoustical qualities and ambience contribution. There are ceiling tiles with plasticized faces that can be washed, but these may not coincide with the design and ambience intent. Fissured or porous ceilings can also pose one other problem. The ceiling should be roll-painted or cleaned at regular intervals. With acoustic tile, frequent painting reduces sound absorption, since paint fills in the pores and fissures. The designer who selects the ceiling surface material should be aware of this cleaning problem, and the merchant who arranges for painting or cleaning the ceiling should consider methods that will safeguard the ceiling's acoustical qualities. This might be accomplished through either vacuum cleaning or spraying on a thin coat of paint when it is required.

One further consideration regarding ceiling maintenance are the ceiling elements. Lighting fixtures, sprinkler heads, speakers, diffusers, and grills on the surface of ceilings collect dust and dirt, as do the duct runs above the ceiling. This often impairs their efficiency. As noted in Chapter 9, lamps (or light bulbs) and lighting fixtures which are not maintained and kept clean will use the same amount of electricity but will deliver a continuously declining amount of illumination. Hence, continued maintenance can directly affect the performance of the store's equipment and thereby affect the efficiency of the store as a whole.

LIGHTING AND MECHANICAL SYSTEMS

While maintenance can increase the lighting efficiency from the lighting fixtures, it can also affect air conditioning costs of operation and effectiveness. Clogged coils and filters increase air conditioning operating costs, thereby decreasing its cooling performance. Both lighting and mechanical systems, then, require regular, programmed maintenance. This means that programmed inspections are performed at specific time intervals to assure constant efficiency and to discover and repair minor failures before they cause major breakdowns.

Actual maintenance programs, of course, are operational in nature, rather than being an integral part of store planning and construction. (This despite the fact that in most large chain organizations, the maintenance department, being concerned with physical plant and equipment, will usually report to the same top executive as the store planning, construction, and real estate departments.) Unless individual stores or chains are large enough to support in-house professional maintenance staffs, regular store personnel will have to arrange for regular, periodic upkeep functions such as cleaning lighting fixtures or changing air conditioning filters. Often it will be the manager's responsibility to arrange with local firms or to contract these responsibilities to outside maintenance organizations. These firms assume responsibility for the lighting, HVAC systems, elevator and escalator maintenance in individual stores or in entire groups of stores.

However maintenance is performed, it is the store planner's responsibility to assure that these systems are easily maintained. Too often, architectural designs make it particularly difficult to clean or relamp the lighting system or to replace or clean out heating and air-conditioning equipment without requiring a series of acrobatics in order to do the job. Maintaining lighting fixtures and replacing lamps are commonplace problems, especially in high ceiling areas such as courts or domed areas and on ceilings above an escalator well.

Equipment areas have been known to be so undersized that the access aisles are too cramped for maintenance accessibility and the removal or installation of parts becomes a difficult task. Rooftop air conditioners have been positioned on the edge of the building with the access panel facing outward, leaving minimal work space for the mechanic, especially when strong winds are sweeping across the roof.

Lighting fixture selection, too, requires maintenance considerations of its own. If the fixture contains a lens, a touch latch should be provided so that the hinged lens can be opened by touching it from the floor. The lamp can then be replaced by a pole. This eliminates the need for a ladder in servicing the fixture. Some stores that utilize egg crate grids as lighting fixture diffusers specify sizes that are adaptable to the washing machines in their food service facilities so they can be serviced at regular intervals for cleaning with a minimum of effort.

PLAN FOR THE FUTURE

Failures and wear do occur in often used equipment and materials. Manufacturers over the years have changed their productions, and thus antiquated their previous items of manufacture.

Stores should be cognizant of this and lay away items within reason for just such a contingency. Many manufacturers maintain obsolete parts for a given number of years. In addition, the availability of certain items such as lamps, fuses, standby motors, and pumps will minimize interruptions of important store functions. Extra yardages of carpet and floor covering to replace heavy trafficked areas are also good foresight, since carpeting manufacturers discontinue certain colors and patterns, and since dye lots may run differently.

Scheduled maintenance, then, is the key to the store building's efficiency in all areas. Design should encourage such activity, making maintenance easy and accessible. Such scheduled programs include group relamping, scheduled cleaning, scheduled filter changes and inspection of motor belts and HVAC controls, scheduled painting, and scheduled caulking of exterior surfaces against leaks. A building is subject to movement; expansion and contraction exist in all buildings. Therefore, there must be constant maintenance to guard against leaks. If neglected, leaks can cause further damage during freezing weather. Freeze-ups, rupturing of pipes, and cracks in the building can develop into expensive repairs. Preventive maintenance, like preventive medicine, helps contribute to longevity.

This, indeed, is the primary point which makes maintenance necessary in itself and a major consideration for the store planner throughout the store's design and construction: if the merchant fails to act until a breakdown occurs, whether it's simply a single burnt-out light bulb or a major air-conditioning compressor failure, his costs of repair or replacement are far greater over the life of the store than are regular, scheduled maintenance activities. The selling machine, the store, is something like an automobile; it must be constantly maintained to properly perform its function at the lowest possible cost. Because maintenance factors are overhead costs, and stores are trying desperately to reduce such burdens, it is even more important for the store planner to recognize those situations where a higher initial cost for better equipment and materials will usually reduce maintenance costs in the long term.

Chapter 15

Plan for the Store of Tomorrow

Every merchant wants his new store to reflect the latest pulse beat of a constantly changing world. But he must be up-to-date, not only on the day he first opens his doors, but on every day throughout the projected life of the store. Plans, designs, colors, fixtures, and equipment are all subject to never-ceasing change in the desires and life styles of customers and in the economics of doing business. The design and construction of today's new store, then, must anticipate the requirements and developments which will affect function, appearance, and the efficiency of the store of tomorrow.

THREE CATEGORIES OF CHANGE

The changes which can be expected, and for which provisions can be made in varying degrees while the new store is still in the planning stage, fall into three broad categories. The first includes the inevitable faceliftings and shifts in emphasis within an individual department, from one to another, from year to year, and even from season to season. This category of change is the one most often served by the elements of flexibility which have been discussed throughout this book. Second, there is the future physical and structural expansion of a department which may be needed to accommodate increasing sales volumes, thus physically expanding beyond the zone or boundary lines of a department. Finally, where the site experiences economic growth, structural building expansion is required to meet the demand. This includes new developments in mechanization which are only a gleam in the eye of a retail planner today, but will be necessities in the future.

COSMETIC CHANGES

Some shifts in ambience and fixture adjustments to suit differing customer life styles, merchandise changes, or store policies, are largely cosmetic and do not require physical or structural changes. They can be accomplished by painting, by replacing panels and other decorative elements, by changing the signing, by altering the focal merchandise displays and fixturing, or through a combination of these. Since most stores attempt to keep abreast or ahead of the times in order to maintain an atmosphere of excitement, and since change in itself provides an element of excitement, these cosmetic changes can be expected to be adapted most often. (This type of change is especially effective because it usually requires little or no construction, physical enlargement of the store or its departments, or alteration in the movement of traffic patterns. Thus the overall character of the store and locations of departments which customers have become accustomed to can remain stable.) Initial design and material specification therefore should consider both the initial costs of decorative components and the additional costs of flexible fixtures to meet the fairly frequent changes.

STRUCTURAL EXPANSION

Expansion and contraction of various merchandise classifications within a department or zone to accommodate seasonal buying habits and to meet changing customer preferences can also be anticipated and provided for both in the store's interior layout and in the selection of fixturing. As explained in Chapters 6 and 7, however, department or zone expansion that results from an increase in the department's dollar volume in sales goes beyond the cosmetic approach. Zone or department expansion based on a modular approach to design offers built-in flexibility without the unnecessary cost burdens which sometimes make expansion prohibitive in cost. The layout of sprinklers, lighting systems, and air-conditioning outlets spaced in repetitious ceiling pattern permits the movement of partitions and fixtures on a modulated basis so that departments can be made larger or smaller or even relocated entirely without major structural or mechanical alterations to the store building.

An increase in the physical size of the store which requires structural change to the building envelope differs materially from the cosmetic or departmental approaches. If anticipated at the time of initial planning, some provisions can be incorporated. Some merchants, of course, feel that, when an existing unit of insufficient size is unable to provide the space needed to cope with the sales volume in its trading area, it is better to build another store than to expand the existing unit. But where future growth statistics indicate that sales volumes will require a larger store in the near future, many merchants prefer to add to the original store area at the outset.

There are a number of basic considerations to be incorporated into the plan when structural expansion is being considered. The store can grow either horizontally or vertically. This depends on the land available. If the real estate is available at a reasonable cost, a free-standing store has its choice of building higher or of expanding horizontally at the present level or both. In a shopping center where land availability may be limited, expansion is apt to be upward. This does not normally involve an adjacent tenant unless a vacancy exists. Furthermore, vertical expansion does not infringe on the adjacent parking area, although additional parking may be required to maintain the ratio of parking to sales area.

When providing for vertical expansion (if permitted by zoning code height restrictions), several costly factors are involved. Weight-bearing columns must have the capacity to support the future floors. Elevators and escalators must be designed for future shaft extension. Pipes and conduits should be sized larger than initially required to take the increased capacity and to avoid digging up floors or tearing out walls. Air conditioning or other mechanical equipment must be placed with care, especially if it's to be located on the roof, where an additional level may be added. Staircases will require an increase in size, since additional floors place greater customer capacity burdens on the lower stair levels. All of these provisions add significantly to the cost of the initial building, and although in a successful store they will more than pay for themselves with the added area and its related dollar volume increase, they can be a horrible waste of money if expansion never materializes.

If the land is available, horizontal expansion is the least expensive way to expand. There is less need to provide oversized building functions or increased structural support to carry the anticipated additional floors. A somewhat larger mechanical equipment room may be an economical preparation for future horizontal additions, but the columns and structural steel need not be any stronger than the initial building dictates. The site characteristics and demands will dictate the direction of expansion. In what direction horizontal expansion takes place depends upon the land available, the grade or orientation of the building, the internal effect on the merchandise departments, and the feasibility of removing one wall in preference to others for expansion. Thus, the architectural design for the original store that contemplates expansion should incorporate construction that allows the easy removal of one wall that is non-load bearing and that would not affect the structural system.

In all considerations for future expansion, whether vertical or horizontal, every store component must be studied. In vertical expansion, for example, if escalators are going to continue upward, the roof of the initial construction should include knockout slabs, sections so placed that they can be lifted out when the escalator extends to the future floor above. The same consideration should be made for elevators and for large vertical duct shafts. Increased sizes in pipes, electrical conduit, water lines, all are more reasonably provided during initial construction than at a later date.

Modulation of component parts of the building, its interior, and its mechanical system are paramount when planning for future change. For example, within a building a partition or wall should be located in relation to the modulated systems. If the building interior is not modulated or dovetailed to the mechanical system, alteration costs will skyrocket. The planner must be aware of the affects such a wall will have. An unmodulated partition or wall may restrict the distribution of air, limit the coverage, affect sprinkler heads, and restrain the intended coverage by cutting off the light emitted from lighting fixtures.

An area that is specifically designed in layout as a boutique or shop within a store that is integrated mechanically within its own confines, but not to the overall floor building or mechanical system, will require substantial alterations when changes or enlarging of the area takes place. If each of the functional elements on the ceiling is modulated, a partition could be located within the repetitious patterns of these elements so as not to violate the function of each. Placing the partition, to be dovetailed between modulated sprinkler heads, lighting fixtures, and air-conditioning diffusers will avoid modifying the mechanical and electrical facilities, unless design dictates, rather than function, require change.

Planning an alteration in a building whose systems are not modulated well provides the added complexity of dealing with the existing building functions. What's more, it can force the closing of the department or even the whole store, when foresight could have kept everything open for "business as usual during alterations."

TECHNOLOGICAL CHANGES

Planning for the "Store of Tomorrow" calls for more than anticipation of merchandise trends and its related ambience, shifts in customer preferences, and the need for more space to accommodate sales growth. These, indeed, are the forces that offer flexibility in the original store and considerations for future expansion, just as the knack for such anticipation makes a successful retailer. But an awareness of the beginnings of a technological revolution in retail businesses and how these advances are inserting a new competitive element must be considered when designing and constructing of new stores: this relates to the increasing efficiency promised by ever-widening applications of computers and mechanization throughout retail organizations.

Already electronic cash registers, or point-of-sale terminals, are flashing all the pertinent information concerning a customer purchase—style, color, size, price—to data processing centers, permitting instantaneous inventory updating and constant monitoring of sales trends. This in turn stimulates more frequent replenishment of fast-moving goods within the stores and consequently reduces the back room space required to carry the larger stocks that are necessary when the transmission and assimilation of sales data is slower.

Already, too, ultrasophisticated warehouses and distribution centers are equipped with computer-controlled, fully mechanized systems which assemble store orders and speed them on their way to the shelves of stores, often within hours of the receipt of the goods from the suppliers. It will not be long before master data processing centers tie together the information gathered at the cash register and the directions given the distribution system—completely automatically. While such systems have been developed, today they are primarily used in huge warehouses largely due to the economies of quantity, serving a large number of stores with a vast volume of merchandise. Now that the technology has been evolved, smaller scale applications inevitably will become economical; and when they do, computer-controlled, fully automated distribution of goods within individual stores will become practical.

Today, most stores are functioning according to the old sales procedures in which the sales clerk is the catalyst who creates the sale, gets the merchandise from the adjacent stockroom and completes the purchase transaction with the customer. Perhaps the least efficient example of this is in a conventional shoe department. Here, after ascertaining the styles and size that the customer wants the salesman must then leave the sales floor and go into the back room stock area, find the appropriate merchandise (which may call for his climbing a ladder), and return to the sales floor before the customer can even try on a pair of shoes. In many cases, several trips to the stock room may be required before a final selection and sale is completed.

This is inefficient for several reasons. First of all, sales efficiency suffers whenever the salesperson is absent from the sales floor, since newly arrived customers may not find a sales person to greet them. Second, space efficiency is impaired both by the necessity of providing aisles in the stock room and by the limitation on the height to which goods can be stored and still be within reach. Both could be improved through a mechanized conveyor system by which simply pushing a button could specify style and size and automatically deliver the merchandise to the sales area, eliminating the need for a sales person to leave the floor. The stock room would no longer need aisles and could utilize its entire cubic content for shoe storage from floor to ceiling.

Mechanized stock rooms, then, will provide greater merchandise densities and productivity. Back room space can therefore be reduced and the forward sales area increased. It will also stimulate greater selling productivity from the sales personnel themselves, who remain on the floor to service the trade. There are many classifications of merchandise which could be handled in this manner. Even out on the sales floor, merchandise could be displayed high up out of ordinary reach, but mechanically available for inspection and purchase through the touch of a button. Instead of using just seven feet as the maximum height available within reach on a sales floor, stores with a ceiling of twelve or fourteen feet or higher can increase productivity by taking greater advantage of cubage.

Presently, most of our mechanization and use of computers aid in the accounting, administration, and control functions within retailing. But it must inevitably find its way into sales applications to help the salesman to improve his productivity on the sales floor and to keep him face to face with the customer. The result of mechanization on store design and layout, besides permitting greater use of cubic content, will affect the reapportionment of area requirements, create faster turnover of merchandise, and provide for a more efficient use of space. This means more selling area in a given size store, or a reduction in store size while maintaining capacities normally found in a conventional type store. Reducing store size also reduces its related costs. But it also means more mechanical systems and their related costs to be integrated into the building functions and budgets.

Such developments will not occur overnight. Initial experimentation will be costly, as it has been in warehouses and distribution centers. But increasing pressure for competitive efficiencies will force the giant retailers to lead the way in these areas, as they have in the initial trials of computerized point-of-sale systems and automated warehouses, until wider use brings the cost within the reach of the majority of stores. The time period of development will not discourage a store opening today, although the facilities will not readily accommodate future mechanization. However, the alert merchant and the alert store planner will be aware of the possibilities open to them as a result of experiments that are taking place. As soon as these experiments prove feasible and economically within reach, they will be applied to new stores by men who are in the know.

Glossary of Store Planning Terms

Prepared by Lawrence J. Israel of Copeland, Novak & Israel.

PHYSICAL ELEMENTS

Adjacent Stock Room (Also called **Forward Stock**). The area immediately behind selling space devoted to stock reserves and an adjunct to selling capacity.

Behind-the-Scenes. All spaces behind perimeter partitions inclusive of selling and nonselling functions.

Boutique. A shop designed to present specially selected associated merchandise with specialty shop appeal and ambience.

Building Function Area. The area not available for store functions, including walls, columns, entrances, stairs, escalators, elevators, mechanical equipment rooms, machinery rooms, electrical equipment rooms, toilets, pipe spaces, ducts, permanent passageways, and fixed building elements.

Curtain Wall. A wall system that hangs from ceiling structure and is normally installed at the front face of a wall fixture to give it recessed treatment.

Double Deck Stock.   Utilization of stock room facilities by mezzanine construction to develop maximum cubic contents.

Dwarf Partition.   A wall system lower than the ceiling and unattached to ceiling structure, its height being variable.

Gross Building Area.   Total amount of area occupied by building calculated to and including the outside building walls.

Net Selling Area.   The space available for direct selling to customer including forward areas, immediately adjacent stock rooms, fitting and alteration rooms, cash wraps, and service desks.

Nonselling Area.   The space available for store functions including show windows, remote reserve areas, receiving and marking, truck docks, storage rooms, locker rooms, maintenance rooms, general offices, employees' facilities, cashiers, etc.

Open Planning.   A planning and design concept avoiding the use of subdividing wall systems (or shop treatment) to achieve a totality of flexible, open, visual, sales space.

Perimeter Partition (Also called **peripheral partition**).   A wall system that divides selling spaces from fitting rooms, adjacent stock, and other behind the scene spaces. The enclosing wall system that defines forward customer spaces.

Remote Stock Room.   Areas assigned for storage of merchandise remote from the selling floor and used as warehousing space.

Shell.   The structural framework of a building including columns, girders, beams, floor construction, exterior walls, and roof.

Shop.   The physical subdivision of selling space into a specific room normally developed to present one department of merchandise.

Shop Treatment.   A planning and design concept utilizing the principle of various physical shops for the housing of departmental merchandise categories.

Soffit.   A dropped ceiling treatment at variable designated heights.

Space Divider (Also called **room divider**).   A physical element to subdivide selling spaces, usually of flexible construction not attached to building structure.

Turn-Key Job.   A total retail facility including structural shell, mechanical and electrical equipment, and all interior improvements, fixtures, and decor.

Valance (Also called **cornice**).   A physical horizontal member at the top of a selling fixture, normally used to conceal a continuous light source.

Aisle.   The space devoted to customer and/or materials circulation within the selling area.

Allocation.   The technique of placement and calculation of sizes of sales departments and service areas within a store plan.

Back Fixture.   A fixture within an island behind the counter line and sales clerk aisle, normally with a combination of merchandise display and reserve.

Convertibility.   A technique of fixturing that includes flexibility as well as the facility to change merchandise presentation (for example, hanging to shelving).

Flexibility.   A technique of fixturization in which the component parts are movable and not attached to the structure.

Counter.   An enclosed selling fixture used for forward merchandise storage and some display—normally used for over-counter selling by sales personnel.

Cubage.   A description of the three dimensions of space, normally associated with the vertical utilization for achieving maximum merchandise capacity.

Fixture.   The selling equipment designed to display, present, and store merchandise.

Fixture Type.   The designation and design of selling equipment to achieve appropriate presentation according to the special requirements of merchandise classifications.

Garment Rack.   A store fixture designed for hanging of coats, suits, and dresses.

Gondola.   A fixture located on the selling floor arranged for self-selection presentation of merchandise, frequently designed to be convertible.

Island.   An arrangement of showcases, counters, and back fixtures to create a departmental merchandise sales unit, normally associated with over-counter selling by sales personnel.

Layerage.   The technique of placement of sales department and service areas vertically according to the number of floors available.

Lighting Fixture.   The instrument designed to contain sources of illumination and to emit such illumination according to a design program.

Maintenance (Also called **Housekeeping**).   The technique of providing cleanliness, repairs, and utilization of all components within store.

Materials Handling System.   The technique of receiving, storing and moving goods within the store facility from truck dock to point of sale, including manual, mechanical, and automatic equipment.

Merchandise Presentation.   The technique of displaying, storing and promoting of merchandise categories.

Module.   A dimensional standard to unify size of merchandise presentation or fixture construction.

Point of Sales.   The placing within the selling space of a highly concentrated merchandise presentation at which position a sale is to be consummated.

Self-Selection.   A selling technique in which customers choose merchandise from exposed specially designed fixtures. This technique normally involves final sales transaction in association with a sales clerk.

Self-Selling.   A selling technique similar to self-selection, but normally associated with a check-out or discount operation.

Service.   All supporting activities within a store operation other than selling.

Service Core.   The concentration of physical, building function, materials handling, and non-selling facilities within a selected store area.

Showcase.   A selling fixture with a glass enclosed section for merchandise display and possibly a bottom section for stock reserve—used for over-counter selling in association with sales personnel.

Slotted Standard. A vertical hardware element designed for the adjustable support of hanging or shelving units.

Superstructure (Also called **build-up**). A movable modular fixture element to organize the presentation of merchandise, normally placed on top of a table.

Table. An enclosed selling fixture generally designed to contain stock reserves, the horizontal upper surface being used for merchandise presentation.

Traffic. The movement of people or goods horizontally and/or vertically.

Wall Fixture. A fixture attached to a perimeter partition for the display presentation, and storage of merchandise. It may be an integral part of the partition construction or a prefabricated case, open or glass enclosed.

Bargain Square. An arrangement of fixtures within a store to encourage the sale of highly promotional or clearance merchandise, usually attended by a clerk-cashier.

Cash Wrap. A fixture designed for the placement of a cash register and facilities for the wrapping of merchandise. Generally located in the consumer sales area.

Cashier Wrap. A cash wrap specifically designed as a station for an assigned cashier-clerk.

Central Wrap (Also called **Regional Wrap**). A major cash wrap conveniently located to service complete departments within the sales area, designed for the self-selection principle, with important decor and signing for quick identification.

Checkout. A cash wrap designed and located to further the self-selling technique, generally located at the exit of sales areas so as to enclose those areas in a controlled customer traffic pattern. Generally designed for a permanently assigned cashier and wrap clerk and prominently decorated and signed.

Etagere. A special modular display fixture consisting of levels or steps of shelving, generally associated with the stainless steel and glass style.

Over-the-Counter Selling. A service technique in which a sales clerk presents merchandise to the consumer across a selling fixture and generally completes the sales transaction.

Selling Fixture.   See "Fixture".

Density.   The ratio of the area occupied by selling fixtures to the total area of selling space.

DESIGN

Ambience (Also called **Atmosphere**).   The general quality of an interior design expressing the store image.

Associated Merchandising.   The merchandising technique in which selling is encouraged by placing related merchandise together within a shop, without reference to buying or departmental administration.

Assortment Display.   The technique of presenting one unit of every available item of merchandise within a department.

Block Plan.   A schematic plan showing the placing and relationship of selling, non-selling, and building function elements.

Contemporary.   The architectural or interior design approach seeking to express a modern life-style and using the wide available range of technological systems and materials.

Decorating.   The art of composing and selecting colors, materials, furniture, furnishings, and accessories to enrich the design of a store interior in creating an attractive selling environment and to enhance the presentation of merchandise.

Design.   The art of store conceptualization including all elements of architecture, planning, interior styling, decorating and merchandising.

Display.   The art of dramatically presenting merchandise to excite and encourage consumer interest.

Eclectic.   An architectural or interior style indiscriminantly borrowing from various historic and/or contemporary styles.

Elevation.   A drafting technique presenting an architectural or interior vertical composition in direct, lineal, two dimensional point of view.

Fixture Layout. A plan which shows the arrangement of selling fixtures, customer aisles, peripheral partitions behind-the-scenes services, and all major elements of the store interior.

Graphics. The art of typography and lettering extended in store design to include all components of identification and departmental background effects including mural painting and signing. The study of written department identifications, including techniques of merchandise presentation with price, size, and promotional information.

Illumination. The art of lighting a store interior, including the process of selecting light sources and output according to a design program.

Image. The character of a store resulting in an institutional personality immediately recognized by the consumer public.

Item Display. The technique of presenting a coordinated group of specifically selected merchandise to promote its sales.

Perspective. A drafting technique presenting an architectural or interior composition in a three dimensional point of view approximating that of the human eye.

Plan. A drafting technique presenting an architectural or interior composition in a two dimensional point of view as seen directly above a floor plane.

Sample Display. The technique of presentation in which one of a kind of a specific item of merchandise is attractively shown, with the back-up housed in a forward stock room.

Style. A quality or mode of design and decoration frequently associated with historic architectural and decorative forms.

Visualization Drawing. A drafting technique to explain a design concept.

Merchandising. The art of buying, distributing, handling, administering, presenting, and selling consumer goods at retail to the public, generally for a profit.

As-Is Merchandise. Inventory normally put up for clearance after a season, regardless of the condition of the merchandise.

Basement Operation. A budget merchandising subdivision of a department store similar to a discount operation and attempting to widen the store image in appealing to a low end of the market.

Big Ticket Item.   A large sales transaction normally associated with purchases of furniture, T.V., and major appliances.

Classification (Also called **Category**).   A subdivision of department merchandise.

Clearance.   The technique of selling inventory at loss at the end of a season in order to deplete inventory.

Demand Selling.   The technique of presenting merchandise for preselected and planned purchases in which location is not a factor.

Department.   An administrative subdivision of store selling.

Fashion.   A prevailing style currently in vogue, generally associated with women's apparel and accessories and referring to highly volatile seasonal consumer tastes.

Home Fashions.   A broad designation of departments within a store relating to furnishings and accessories for the home including hard and soft goods.

Impulse Selling.   The technique of presenting merchandise at high traffic locations to stimulate unplanned purchases.

Lineage.   The length of fixtures measured on the floor plan, normally associated with calculations of merchandising capacity.

Margin.   The excess of sales over the cost of sales.

Markdown.   Total reductions from the originally set retail price of merchandise.

Market.   A portion of the consumer public whose taste, life-style, purchasing power, and economic standards can be defined.

Merchandise mix.   The arrangement of classifications or departments of merchandise so as to produce a balanced sales presentation or, alternatively, a special store character.

Operations.   A generic term expressing all of the service processes of retail selling.

Outpost.   A small presentation of a merchandise classification remote from its parent department and often duplicating that merchandise.

Profit. The excess of sales over the cost of sales including all administration and overhead. Extended to pre-tax or after-tax profit.

Promotion. The technique of stimulating sales by advertising, display, selecting, and presentation of merchandise.

Ready-to-Wear. Prestyled and prefabricated apparel presented according to size and type of consumer including misses, women's, men's, and children's.

Retail. The process of selling merchandise directly to the consumer.

Returns. Merchandise brought back by customers.

Sales Production. The annual volume of earnings divided by gross sales area.

Sales Volume. The annual gross earnings at retail.

Shrinkage. The loss of inventory at retail caused by stealing, inefficiency, and administration errors.

Simplified Selling. The technique of merchandise presentation depending upon self-selection.

Trading-Down. The technique of lowering the image of a store by cheapening merchandise selections and presentations and appealing to the lower sector of a market.

Trading-Up. The technique of raising the image of a store by improving merchandise selections and presentations and appealing to the upper sector of a market.

Transaction. The completion of a retail sale.

Turnover. The ratio of net sales per year divided by average inventory at retail.

Volume. See "Sales Volume".

Wholesale. The process of buying or jobbing merchandise from point of manufacture and selling to a retail operation.

Index